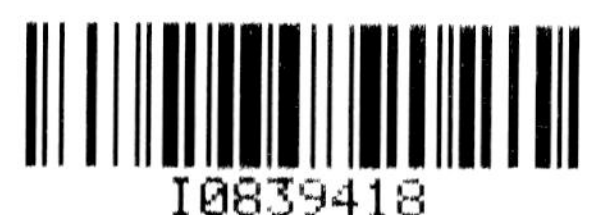

Coloring book for adults and kids amazing Dolphin image for design

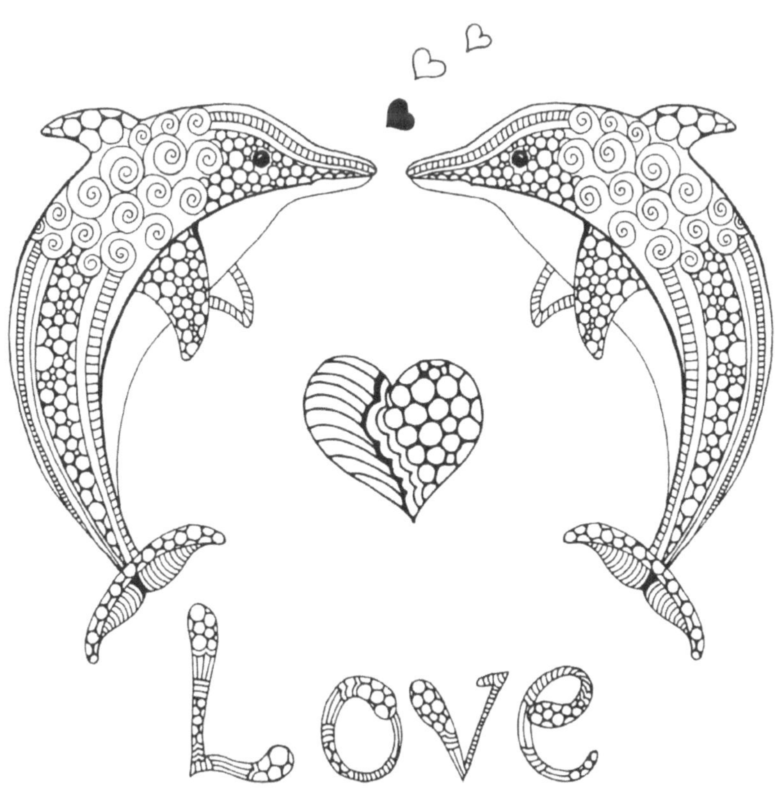

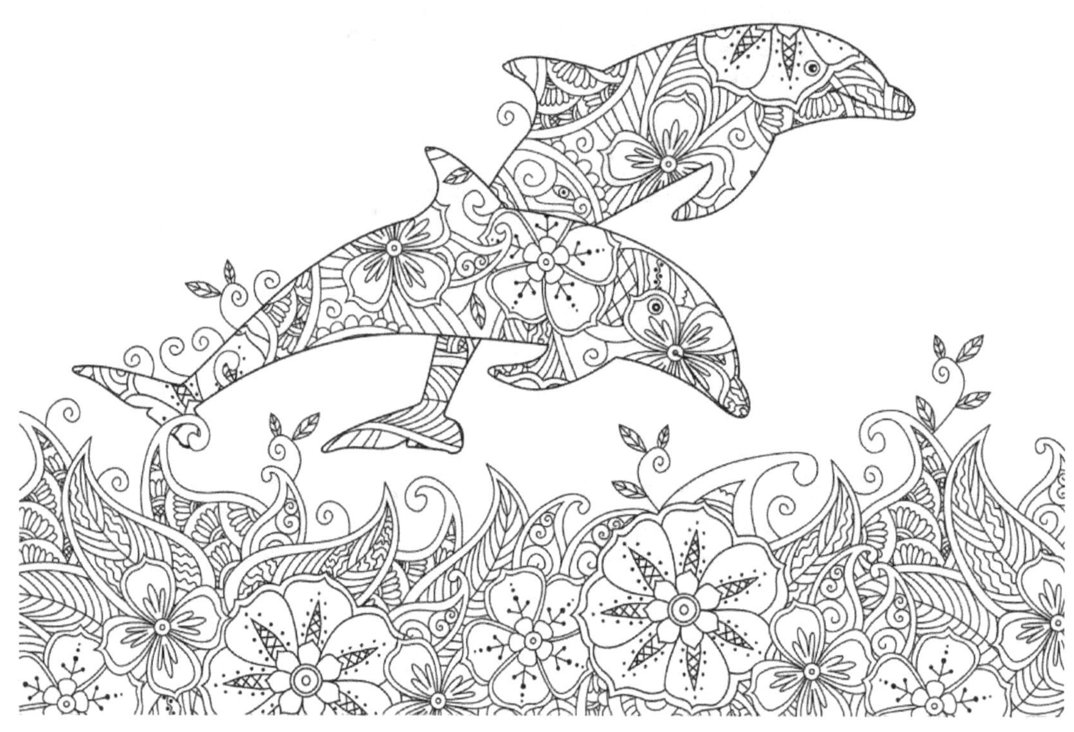

This coloring book is belongs to

____

____

____

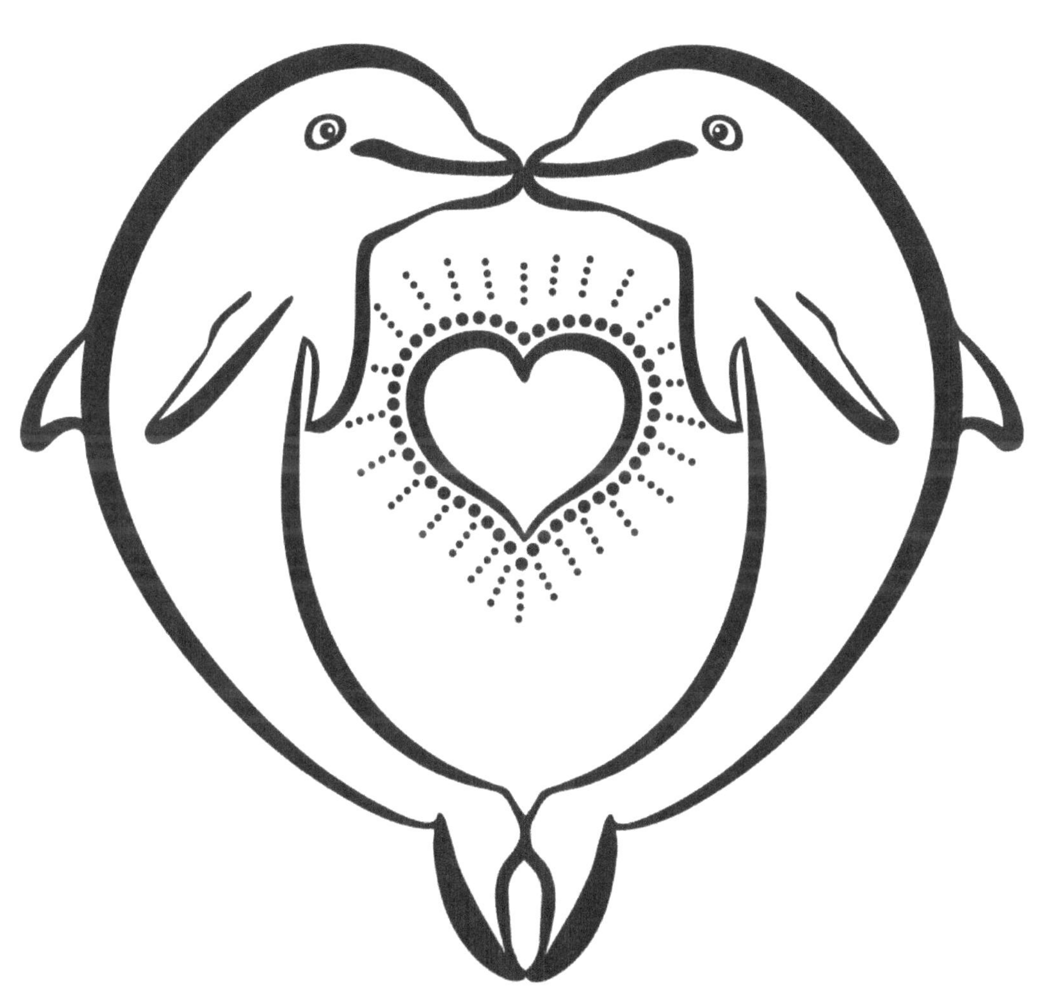

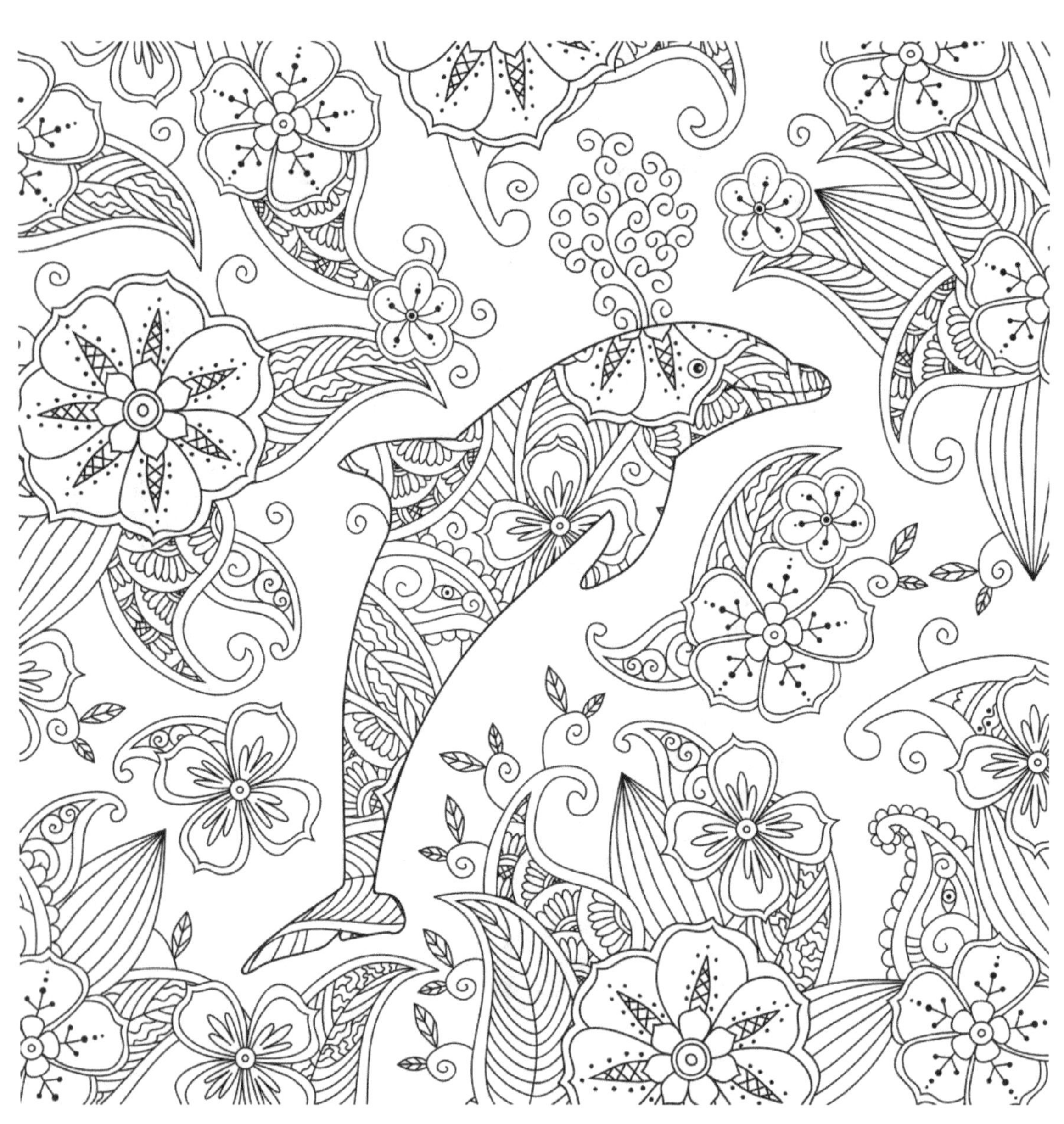

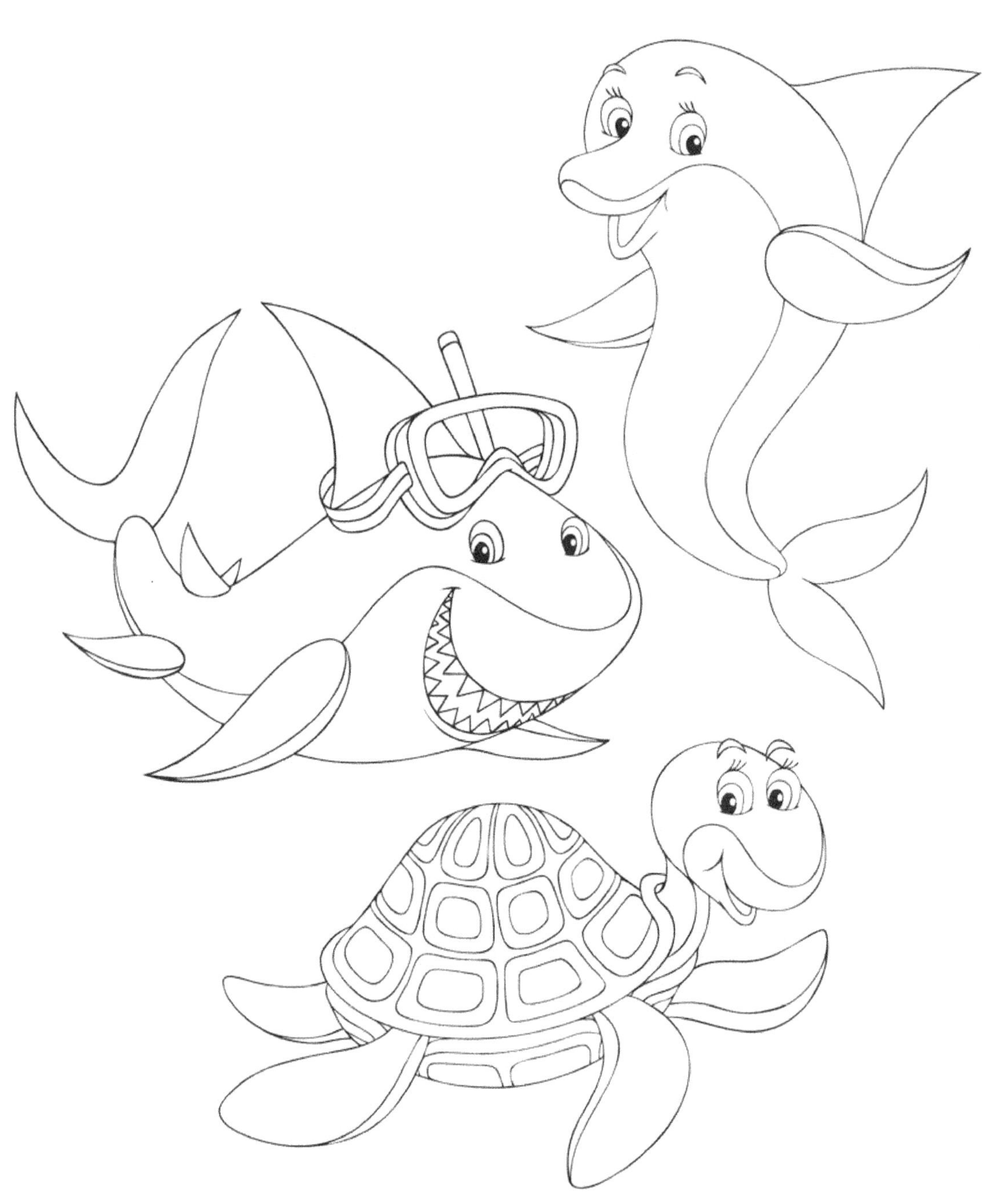

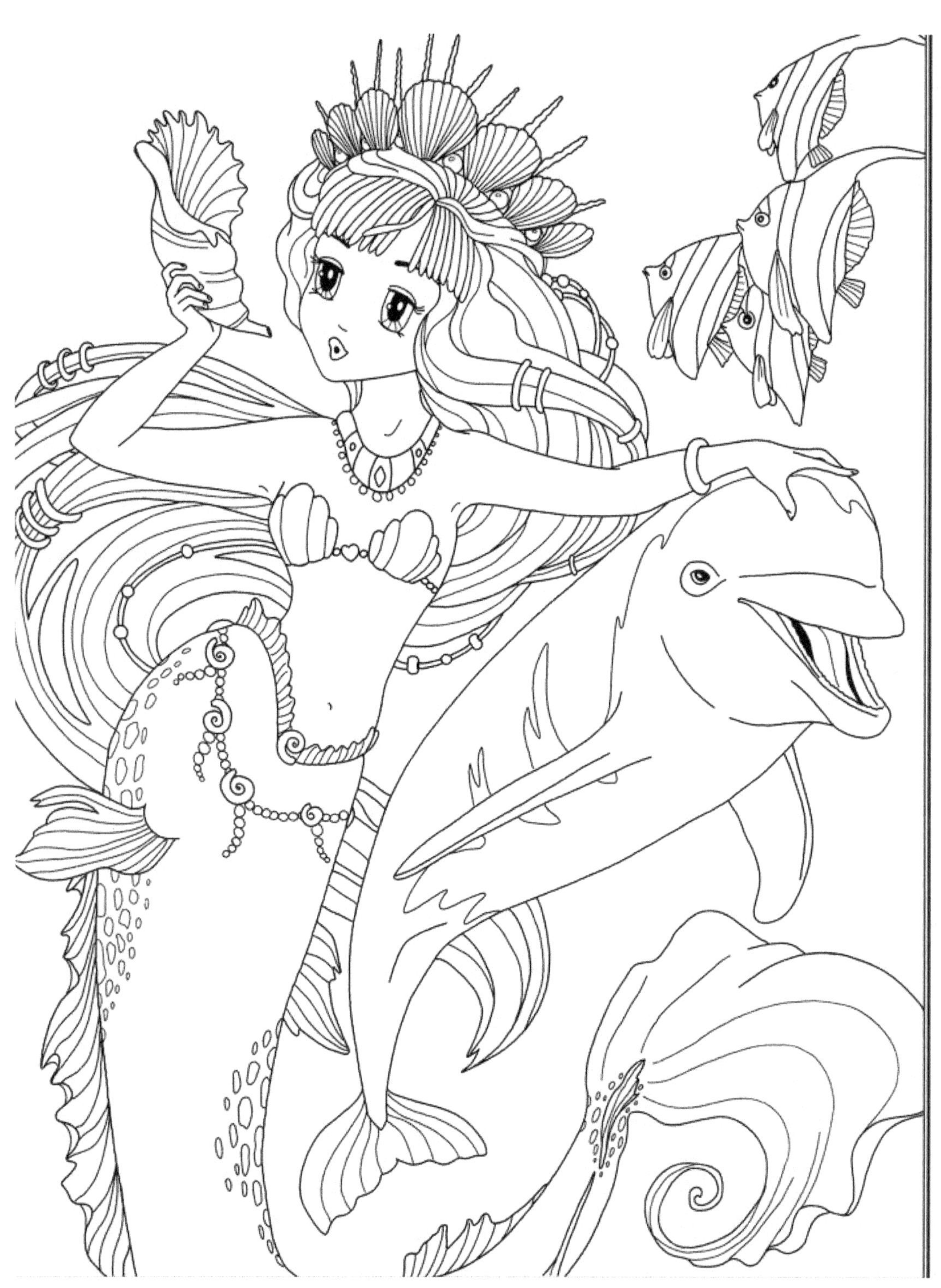

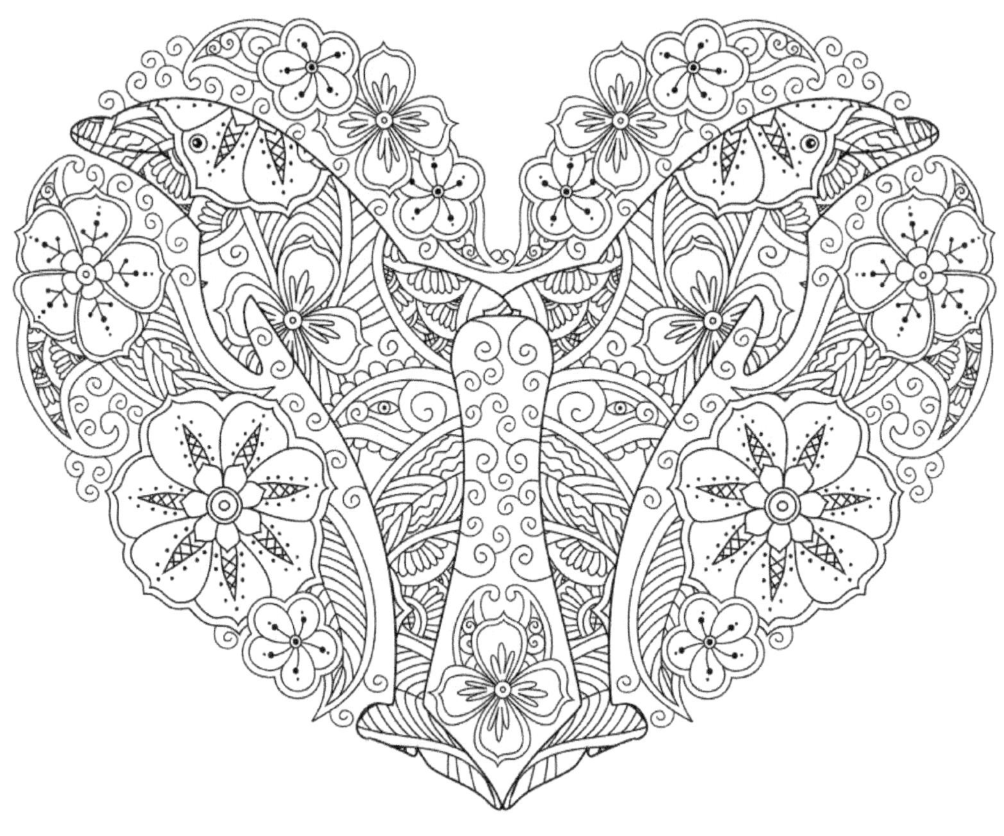

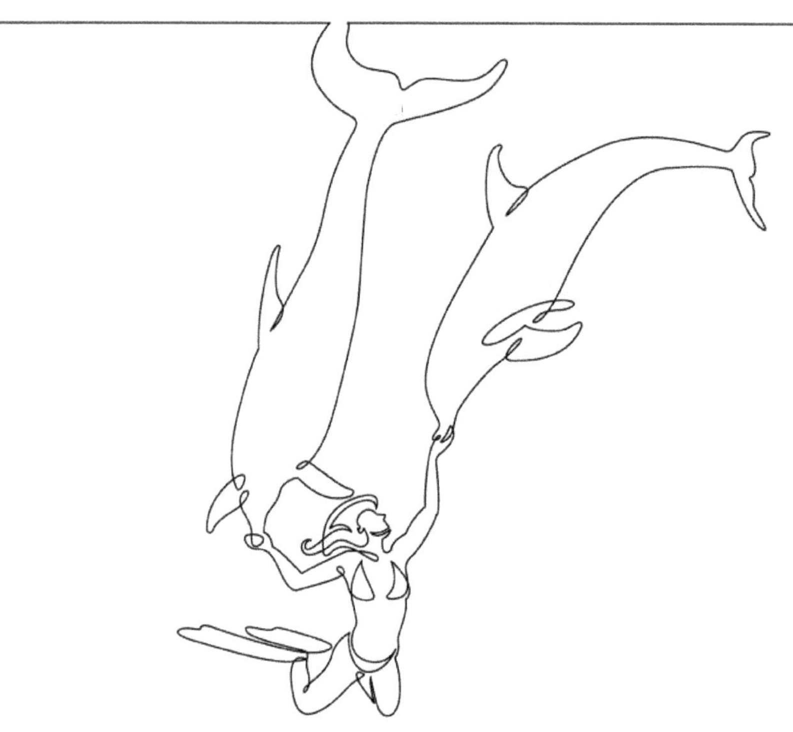

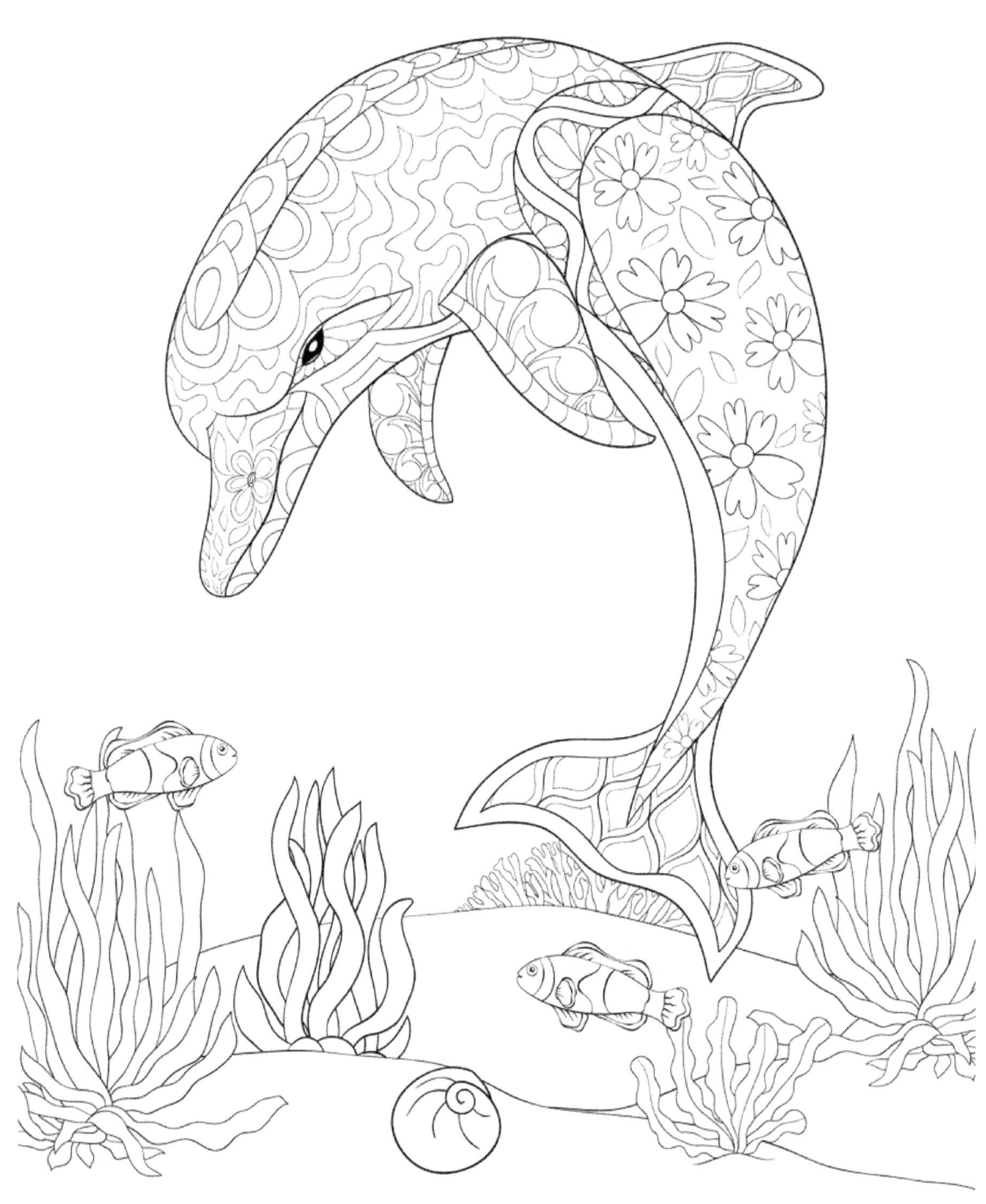

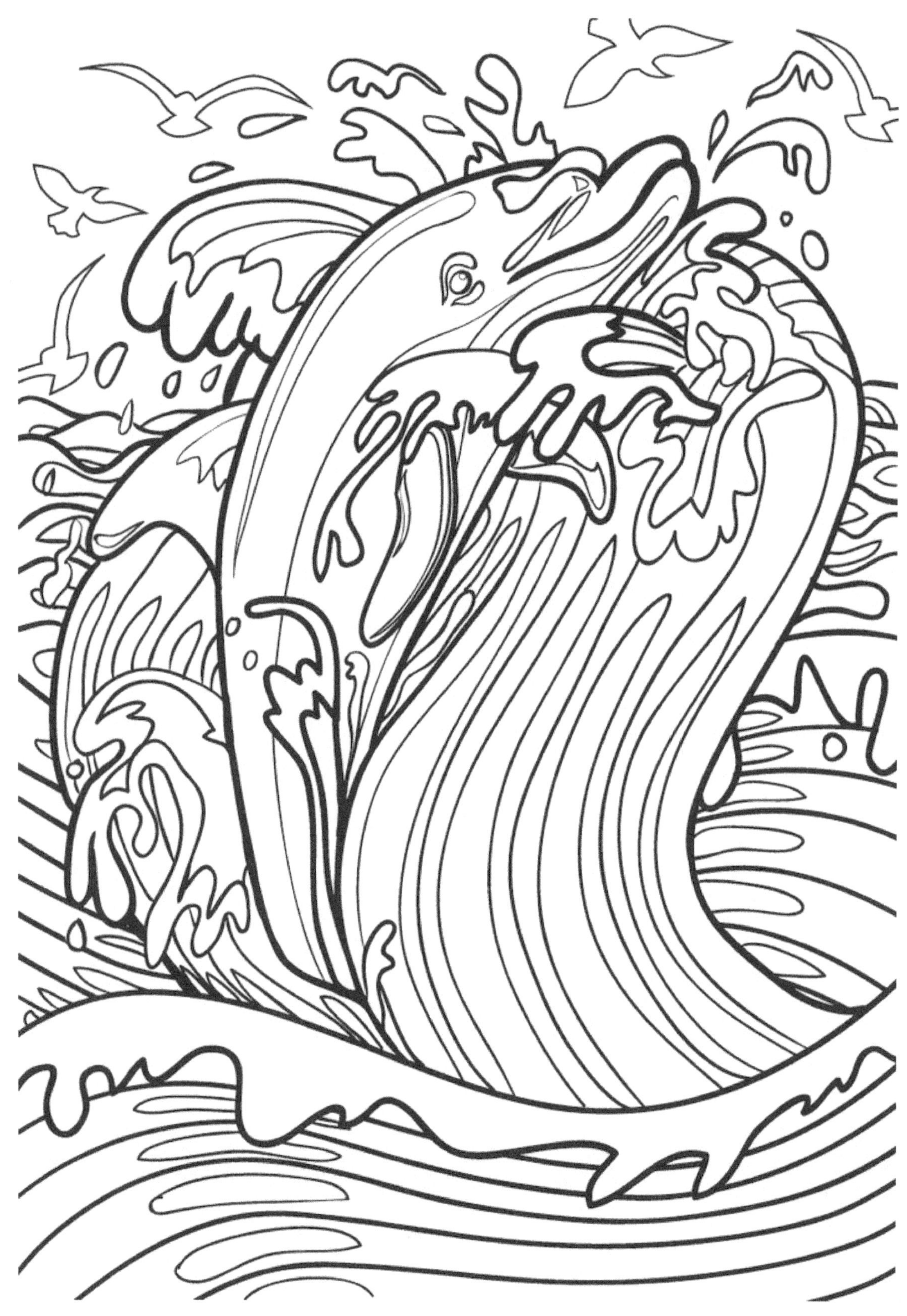

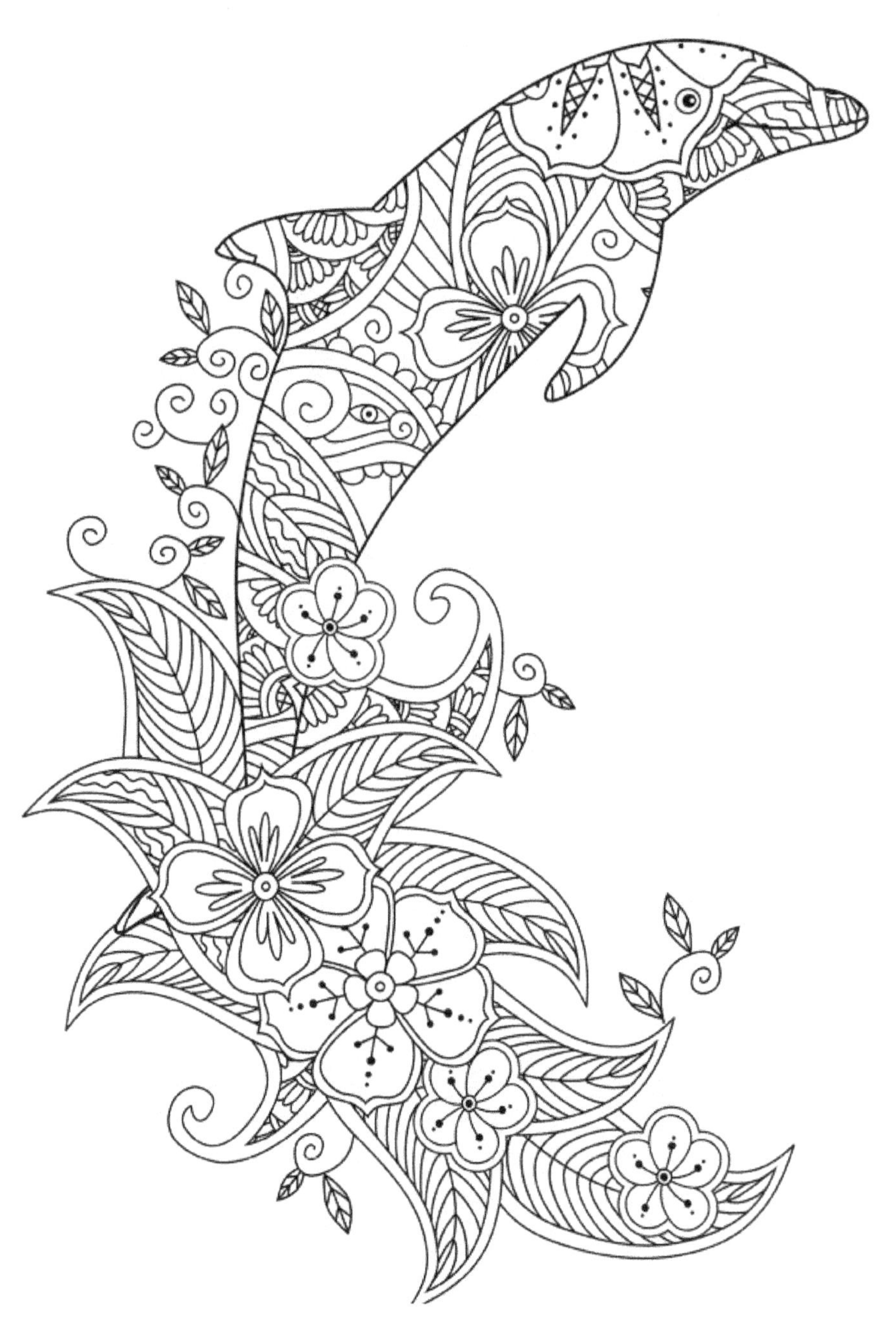

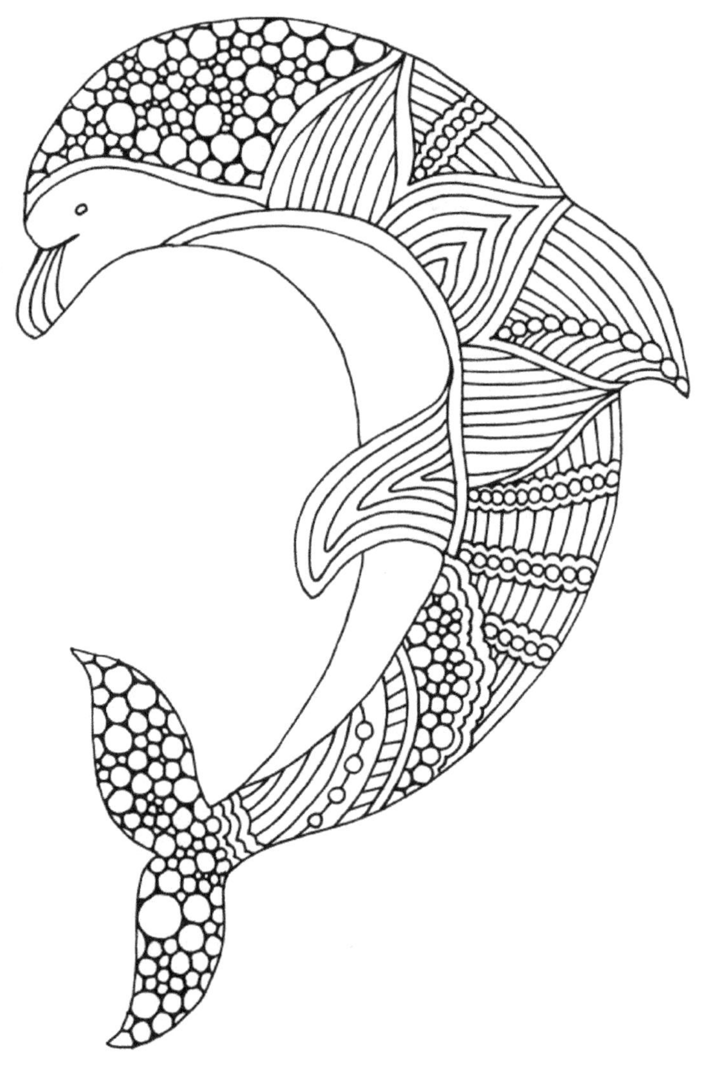

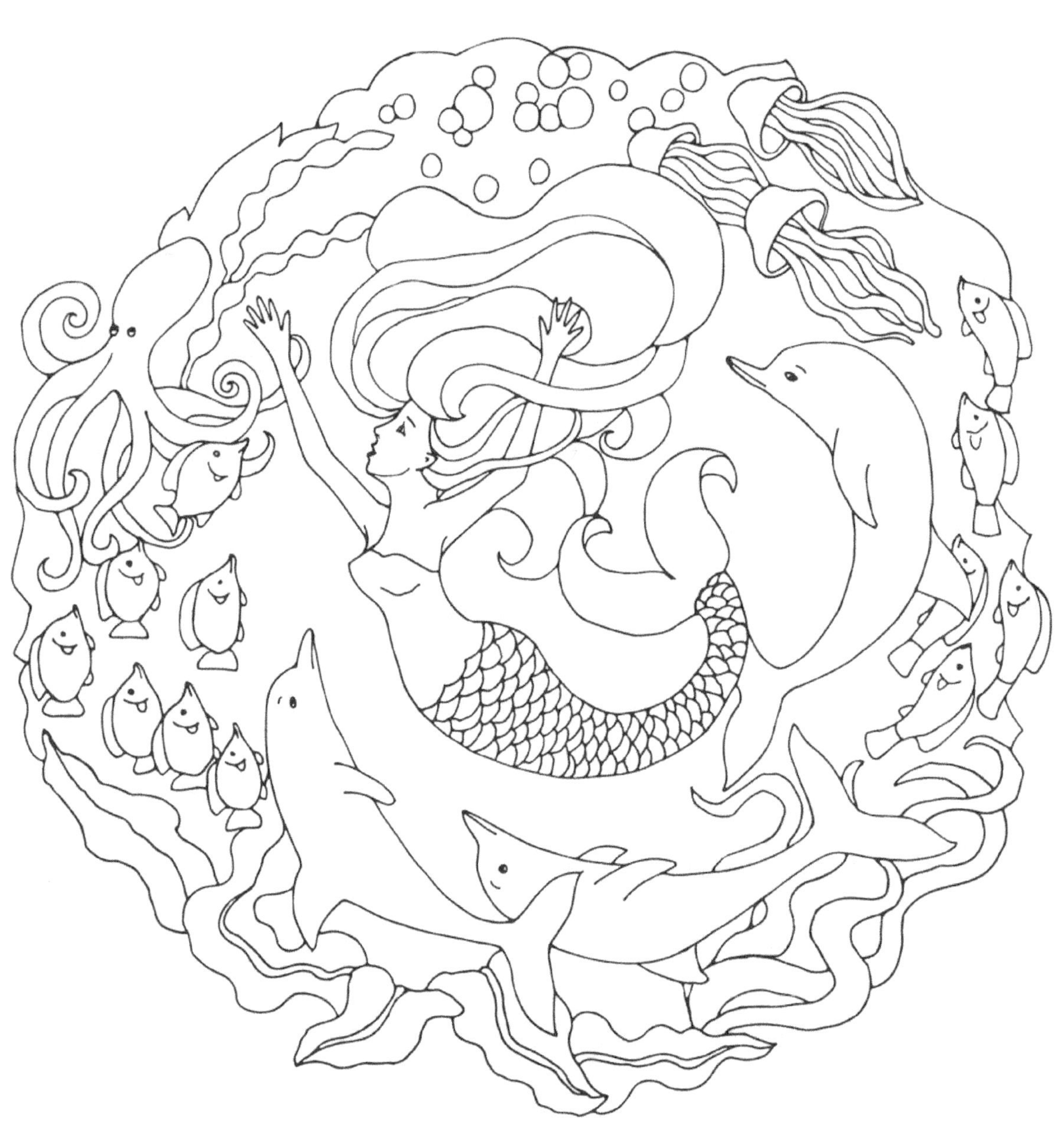

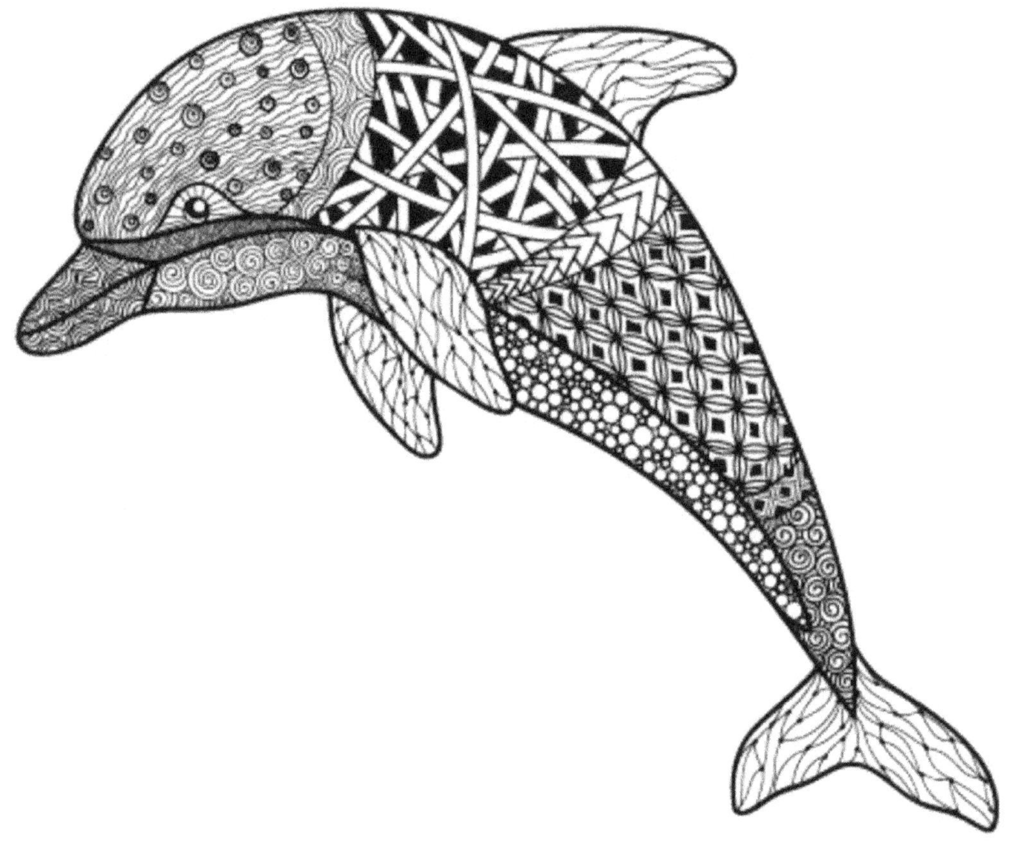

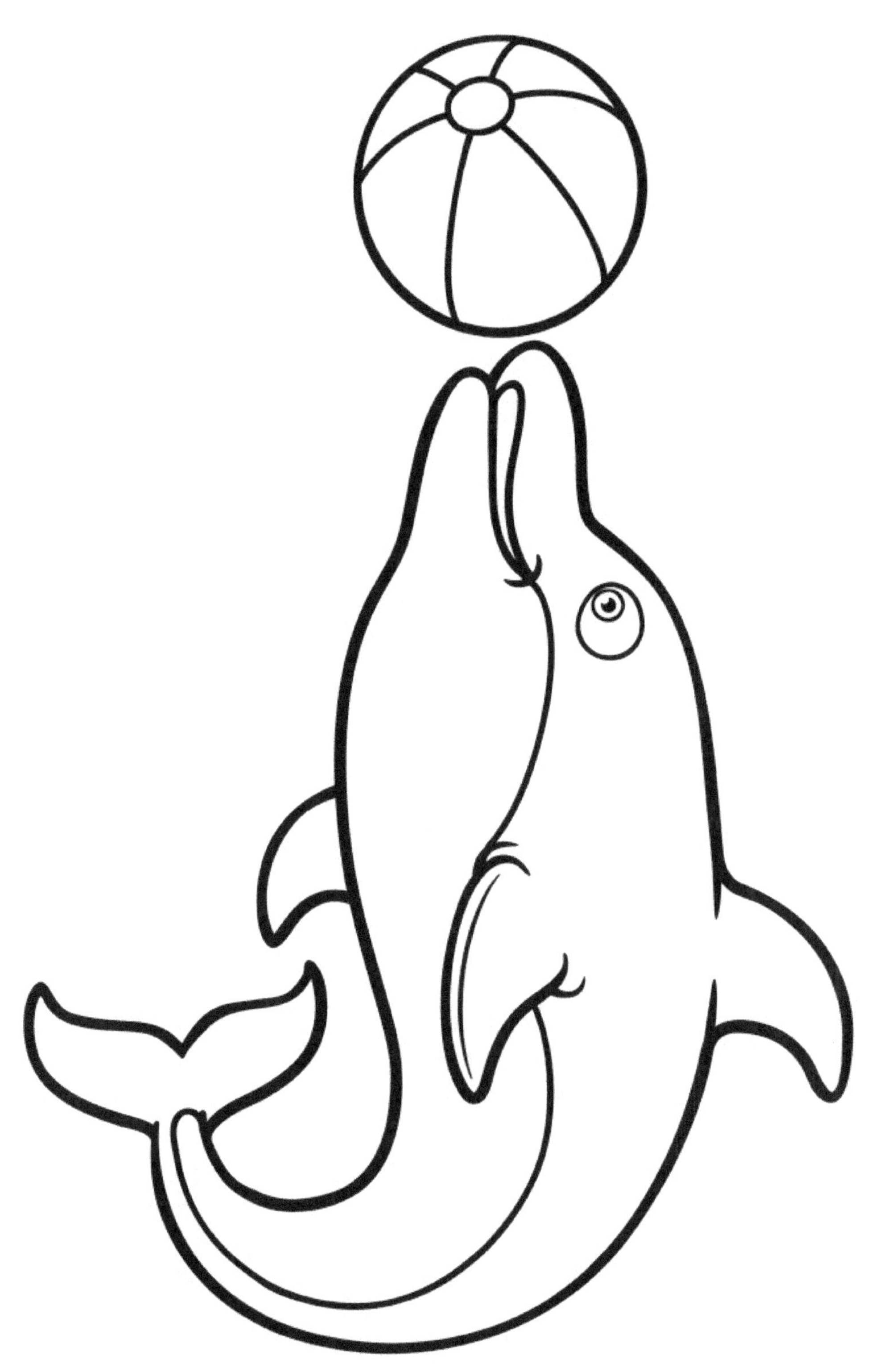

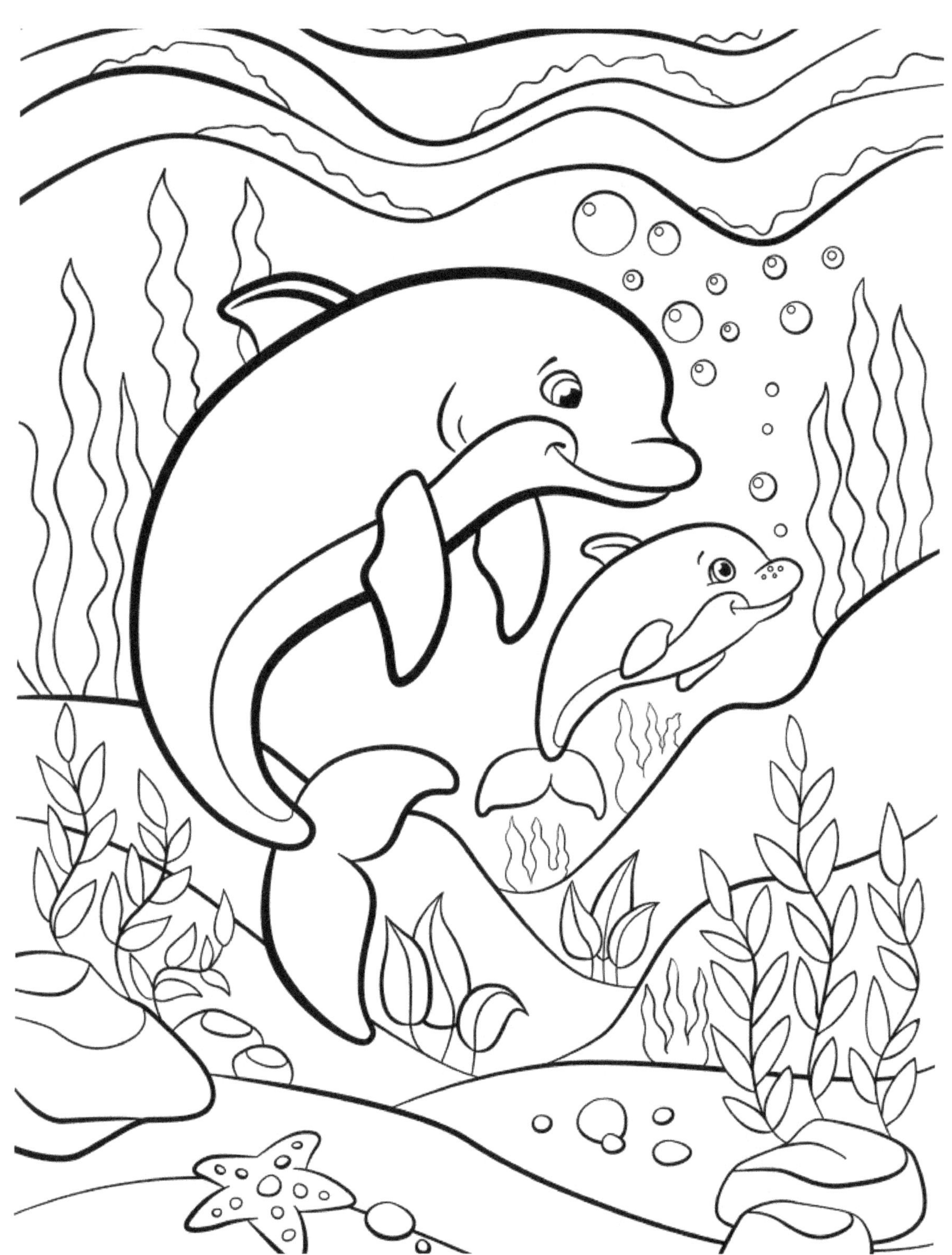

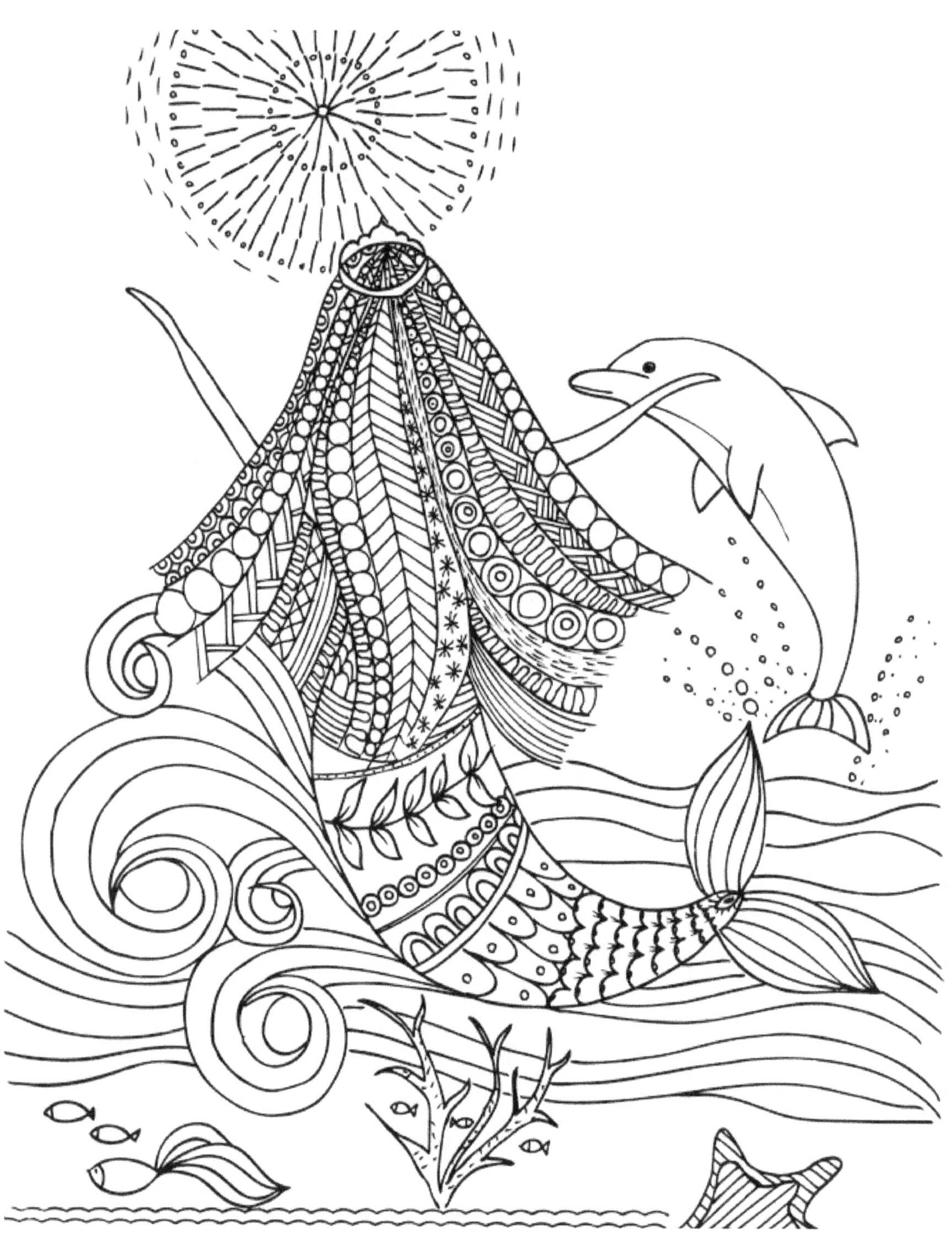

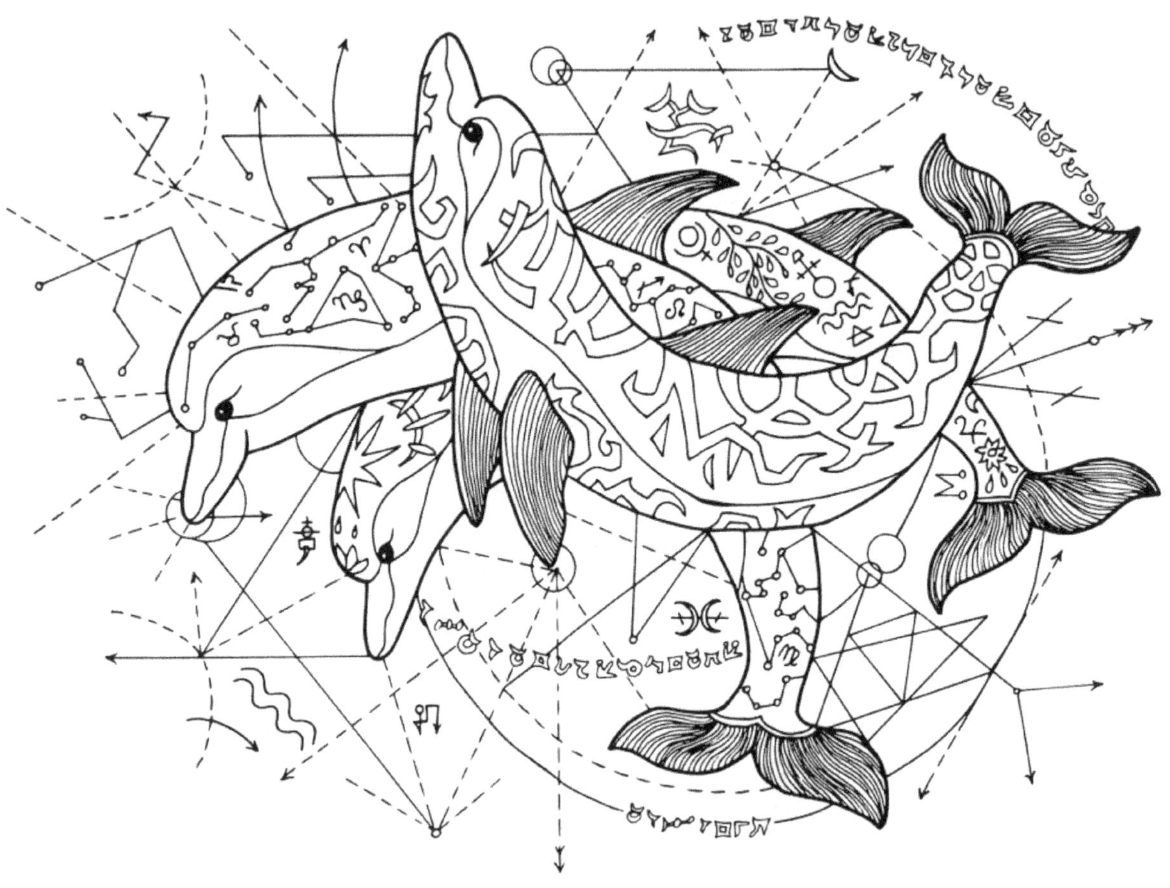

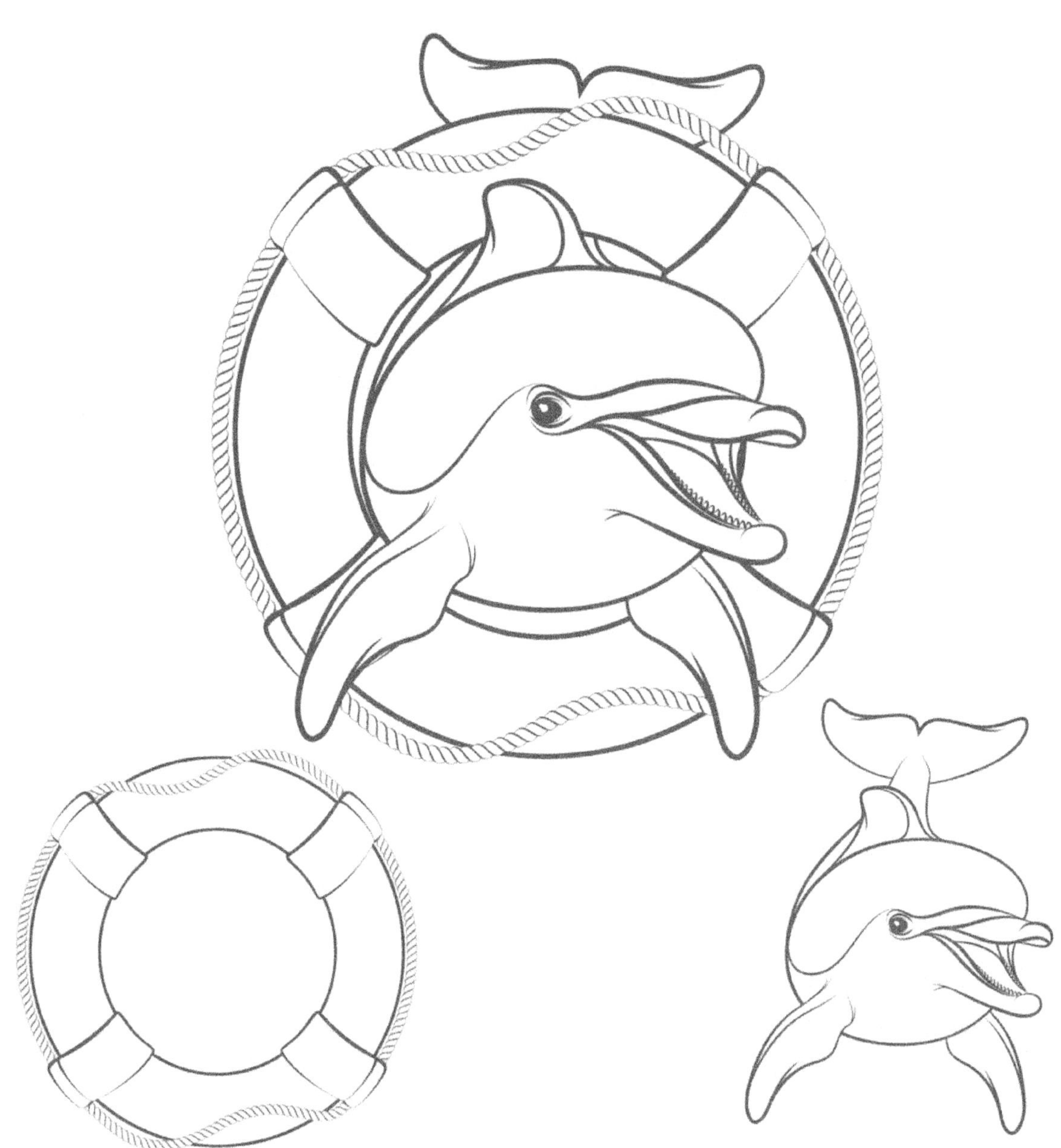

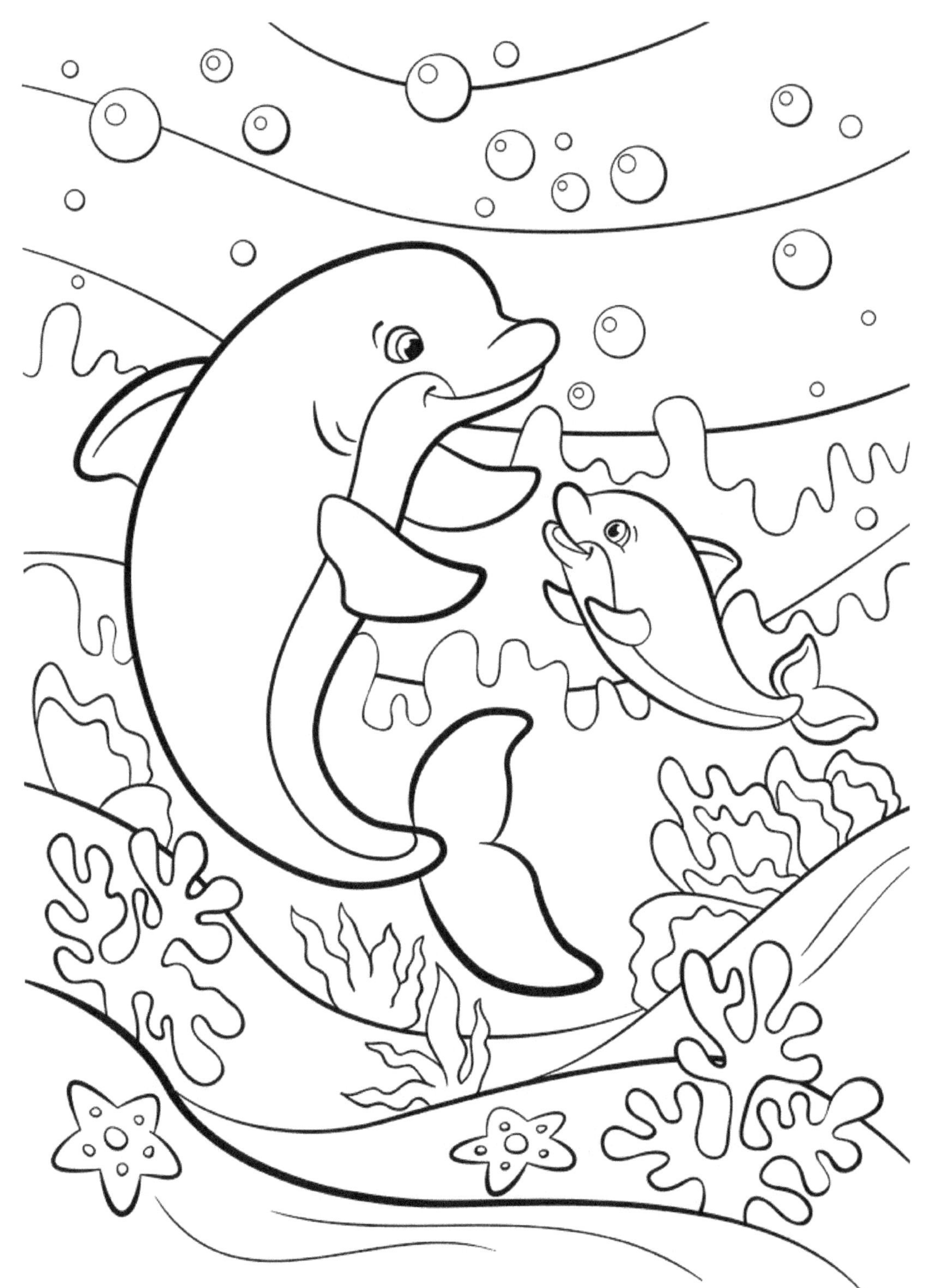

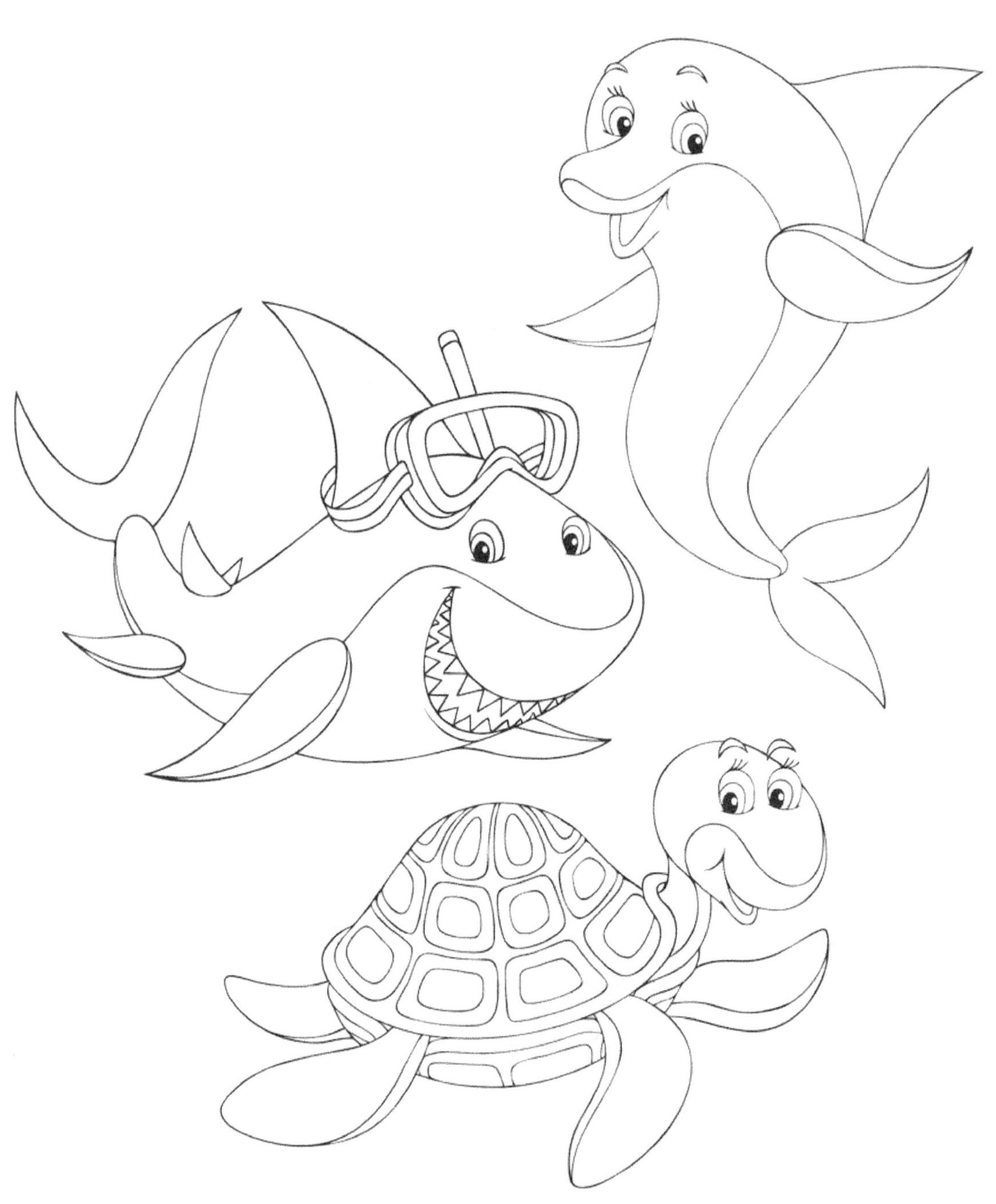

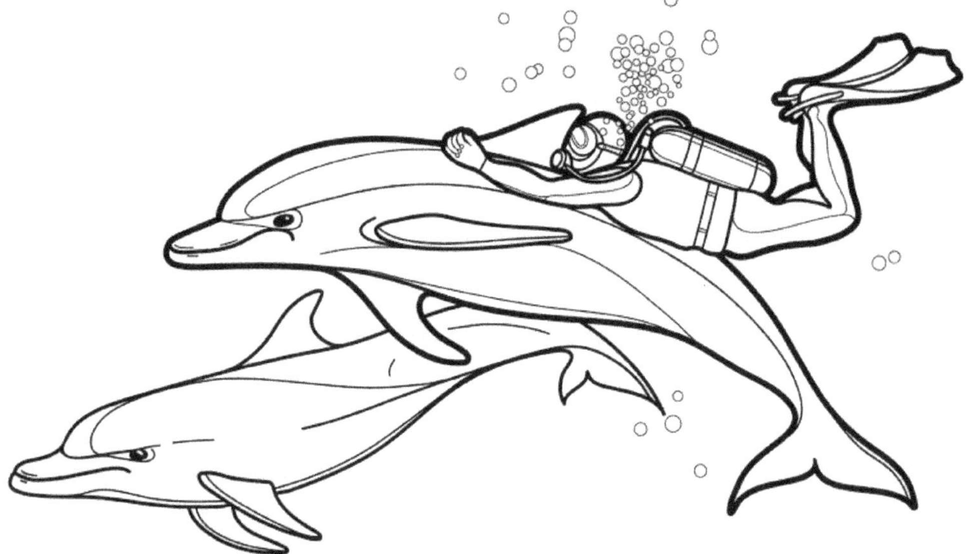

Swim
with
Dolphins

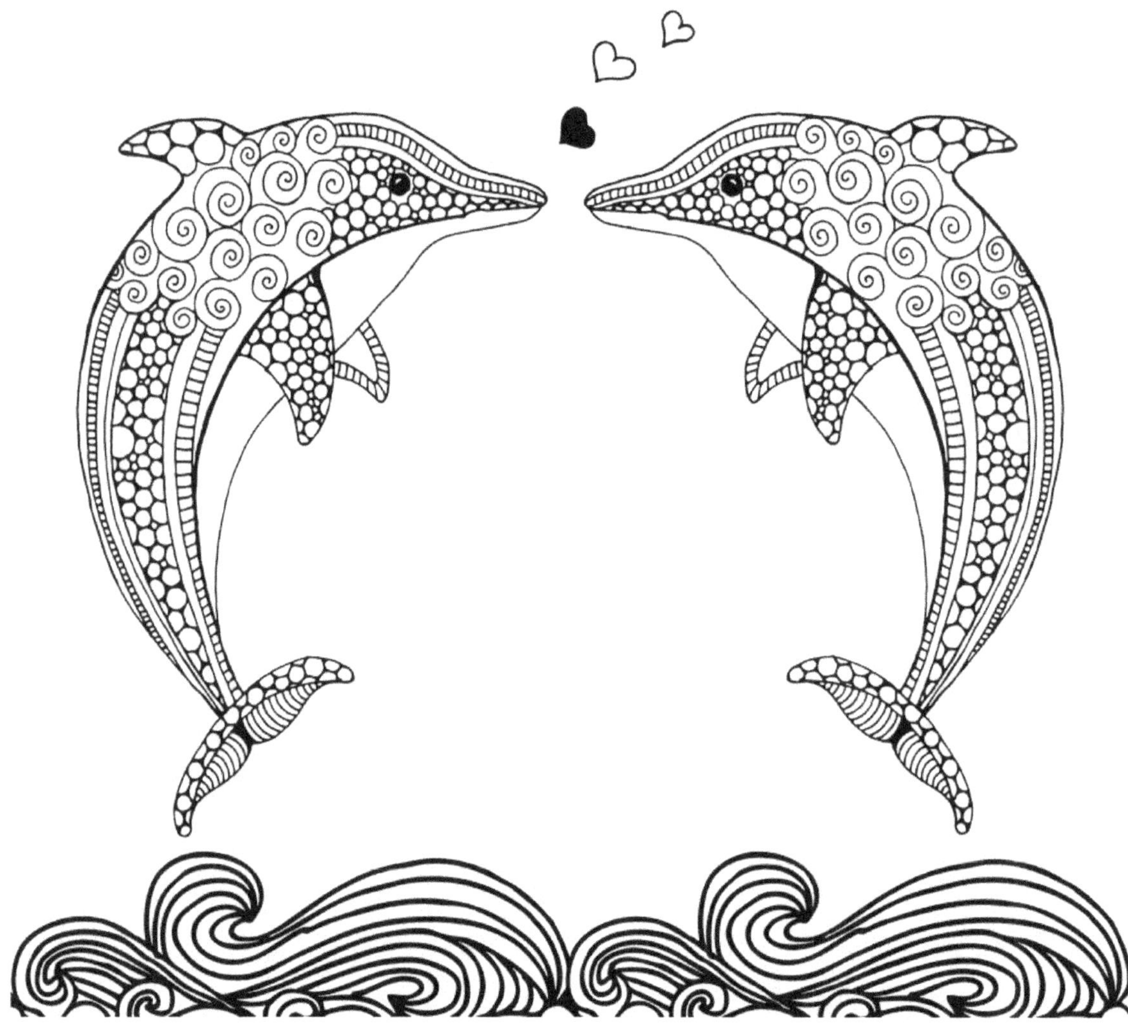

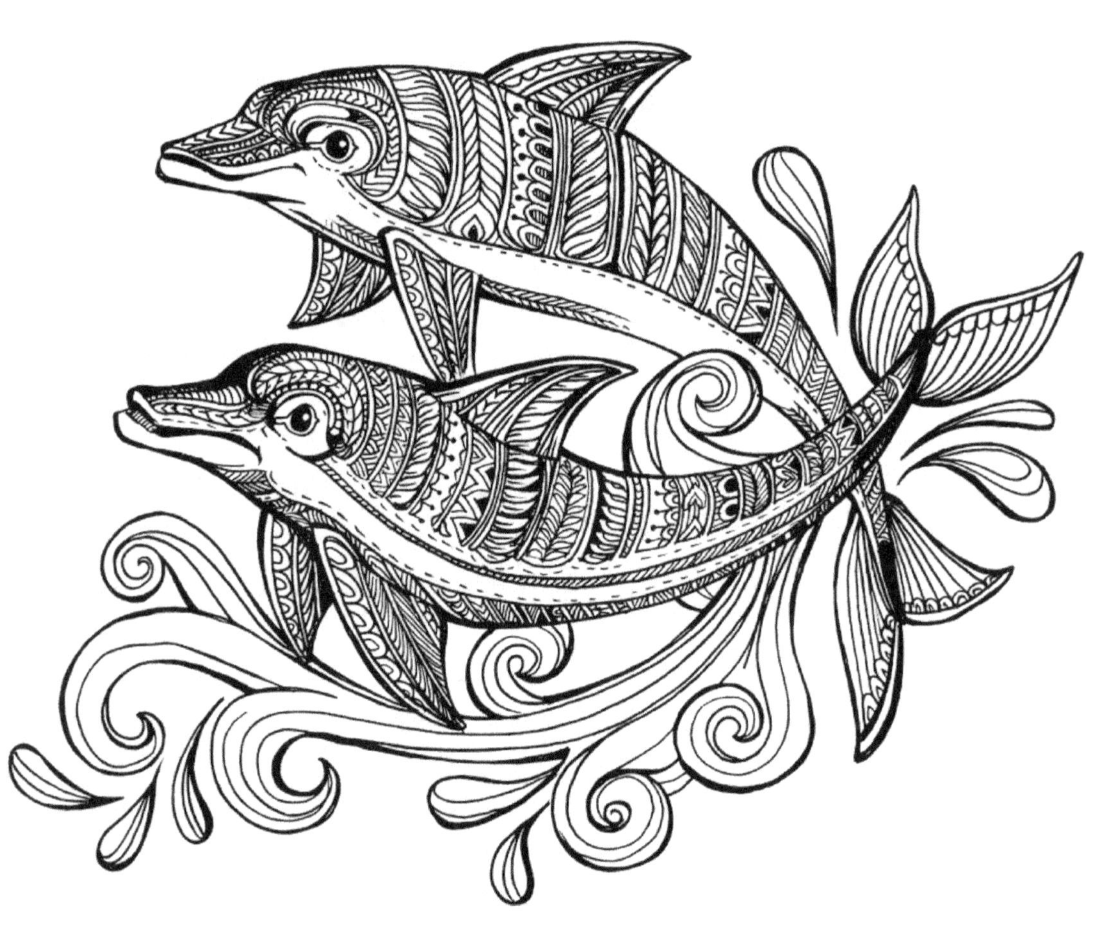

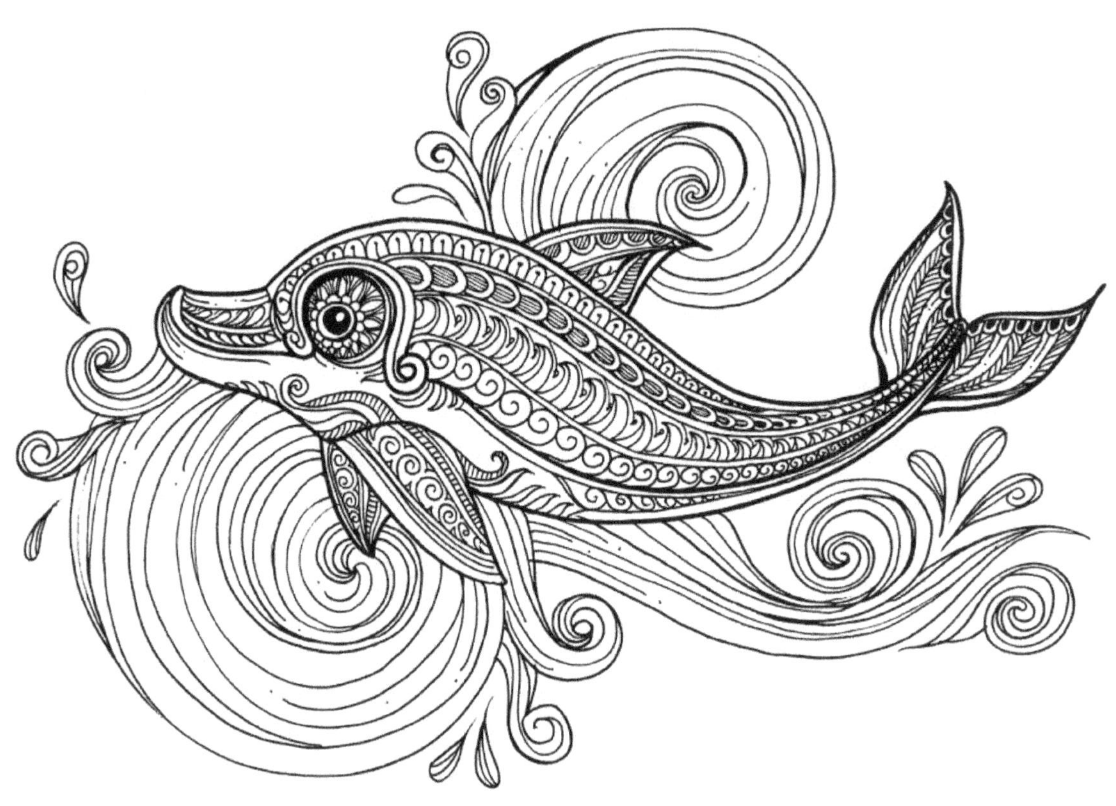

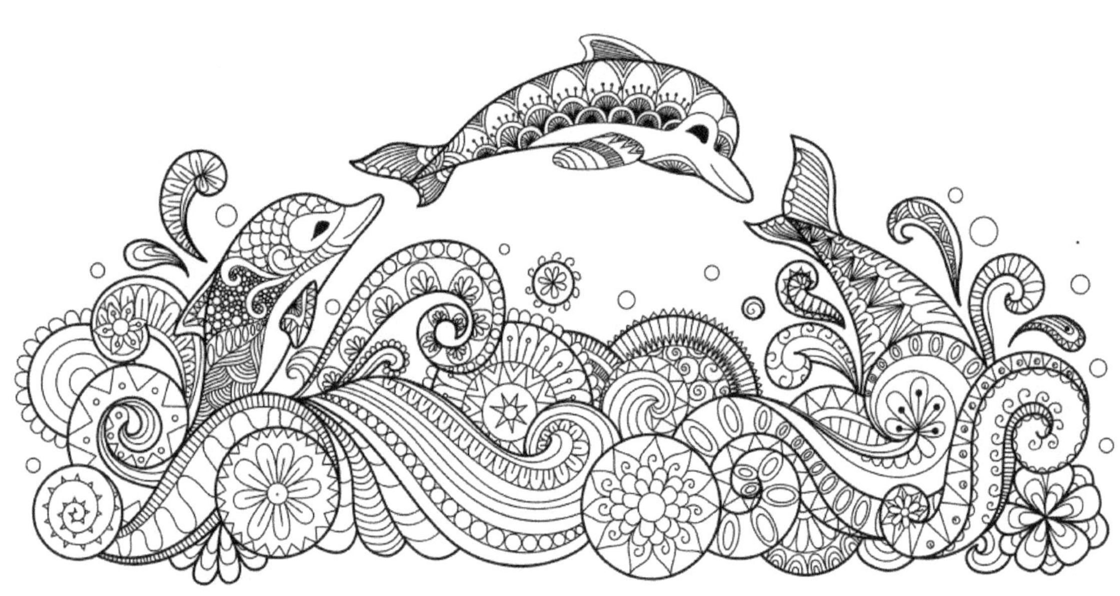

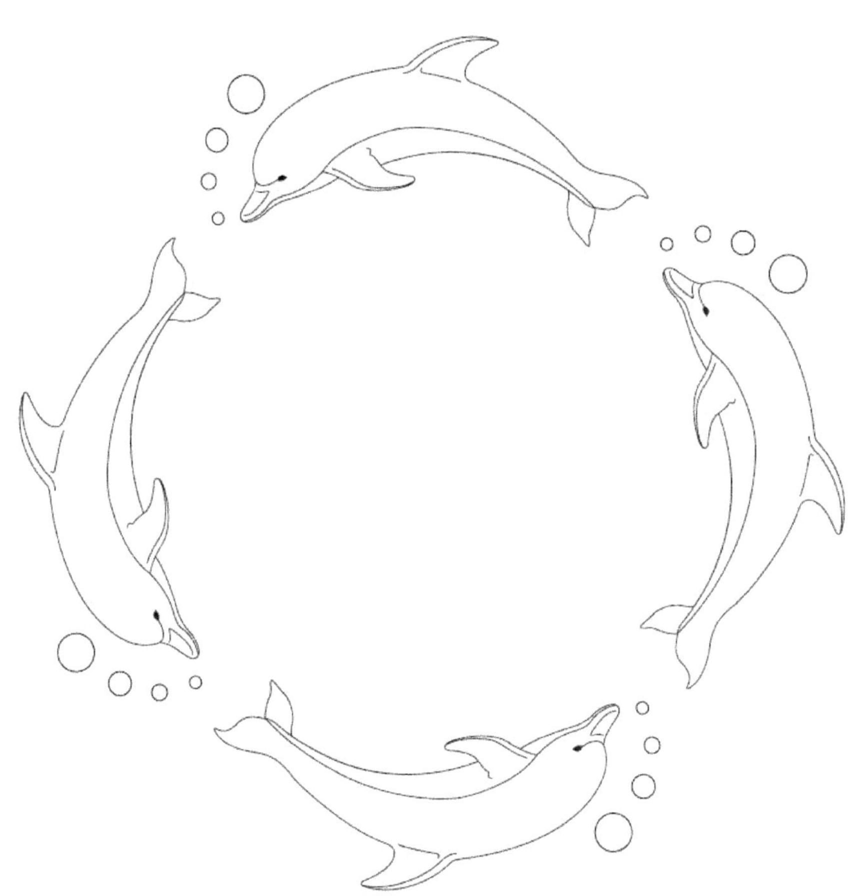

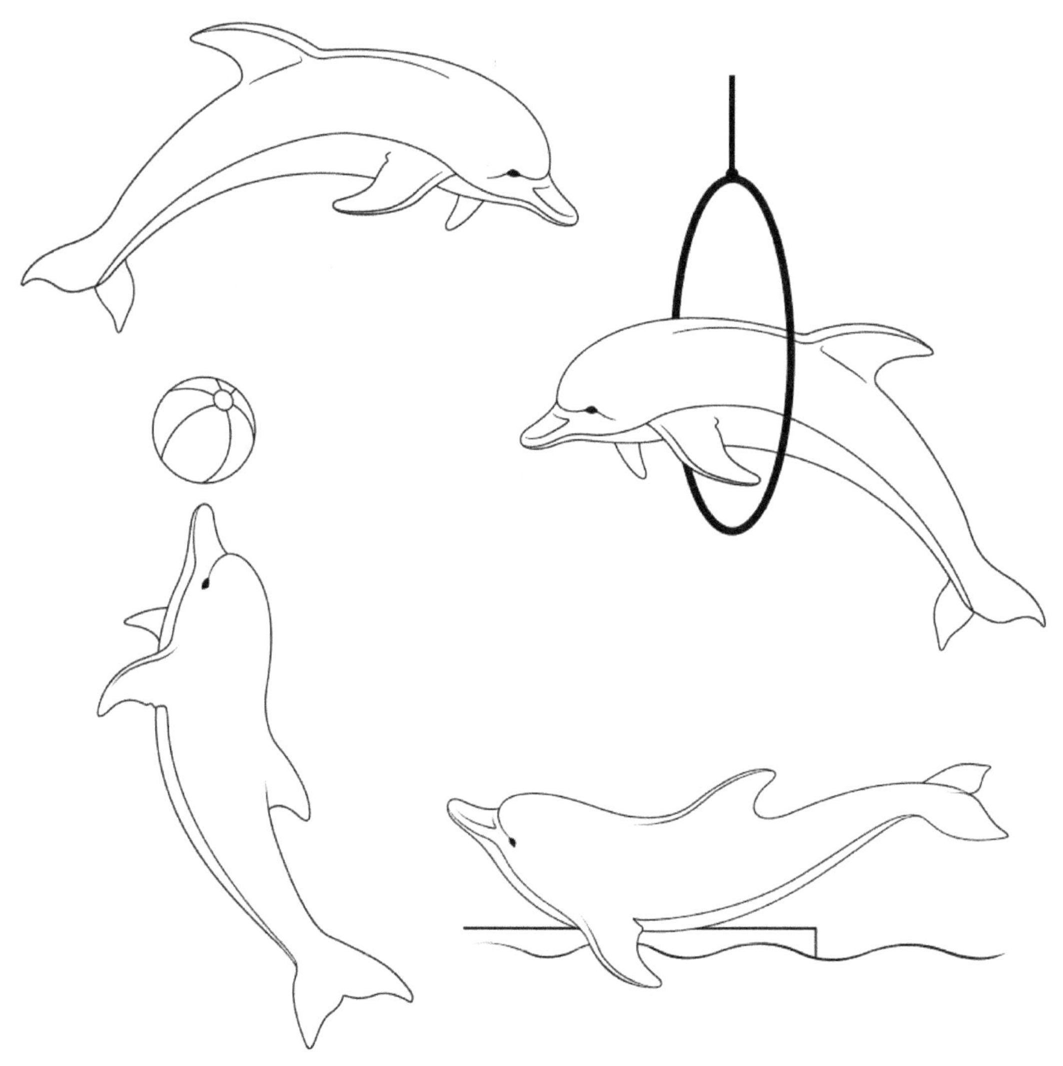

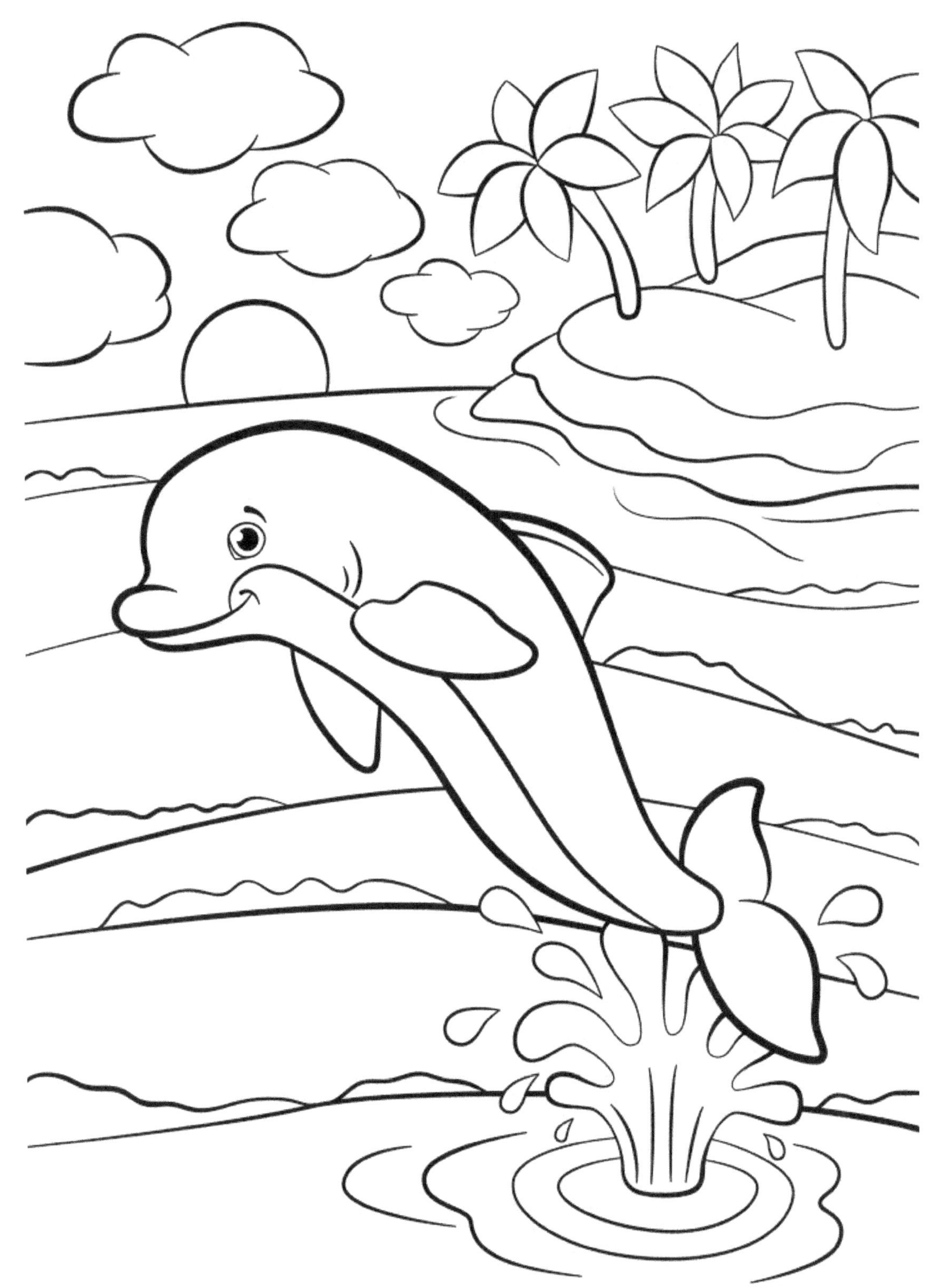

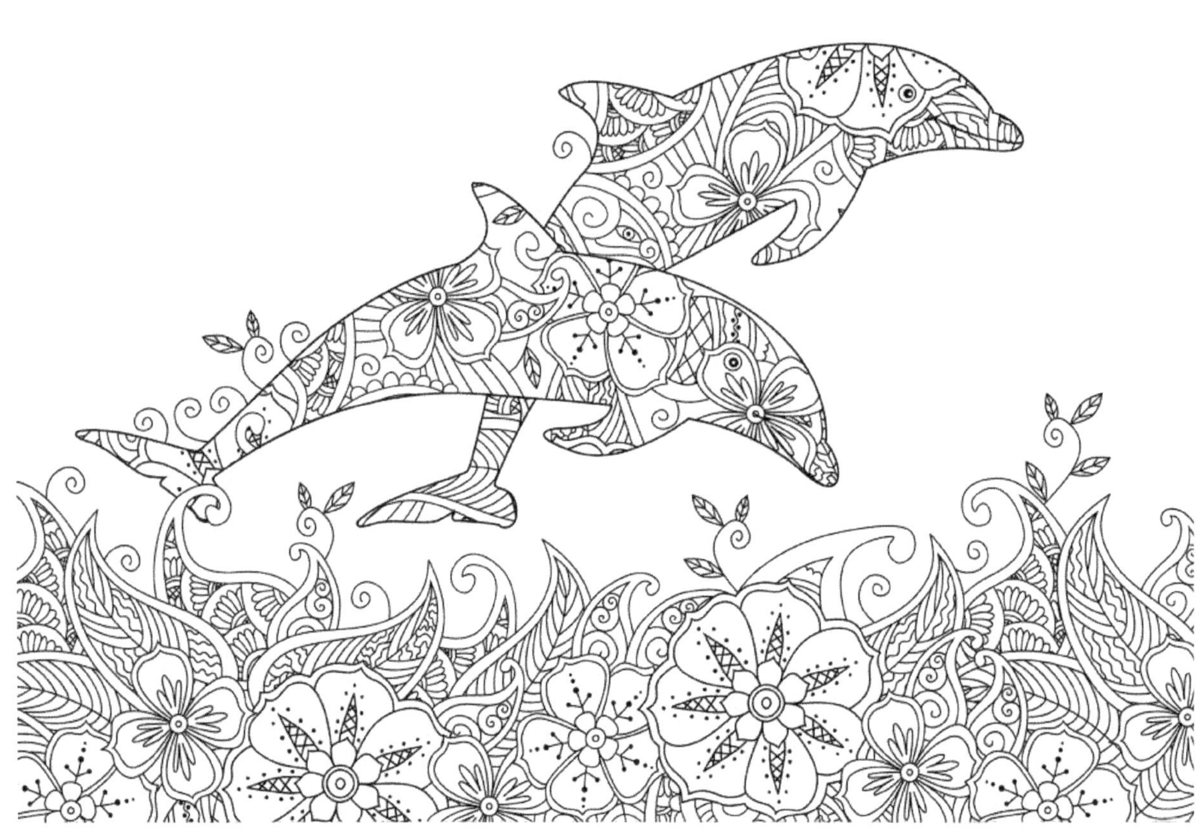

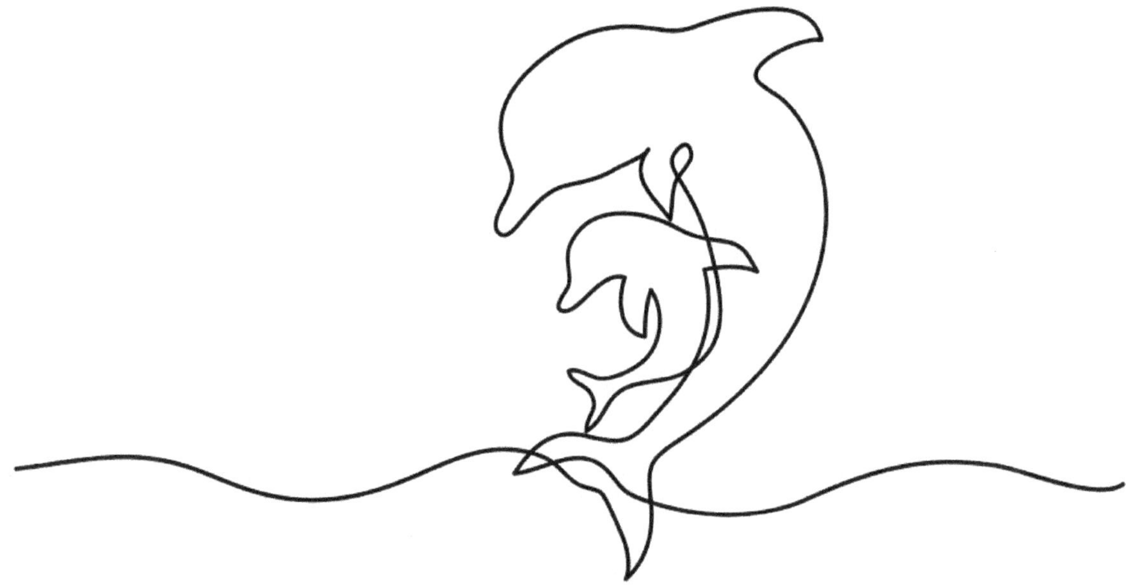

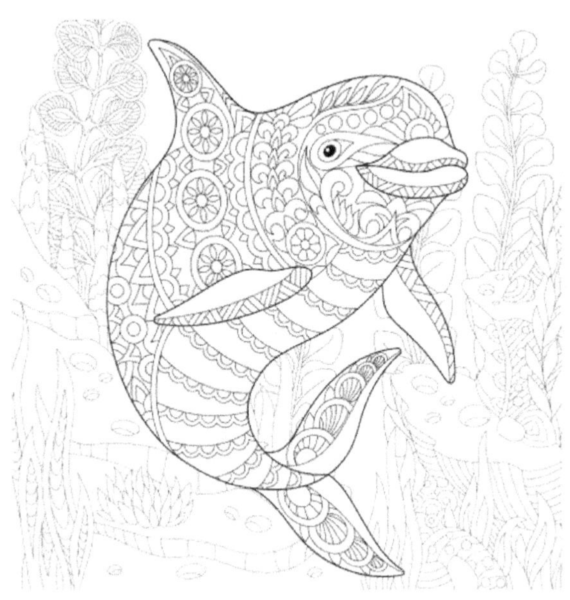 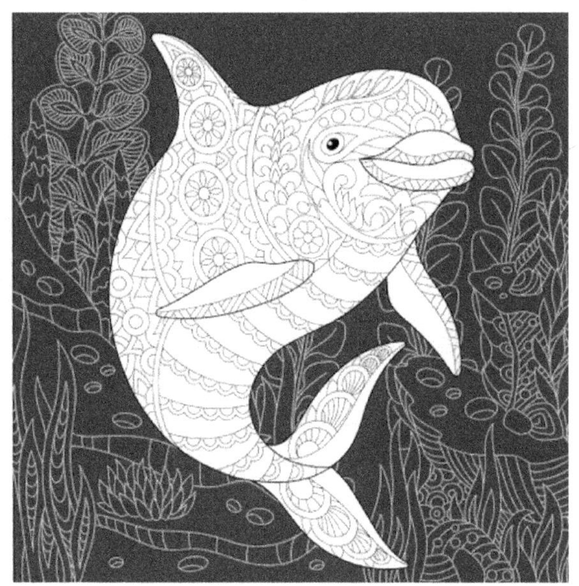

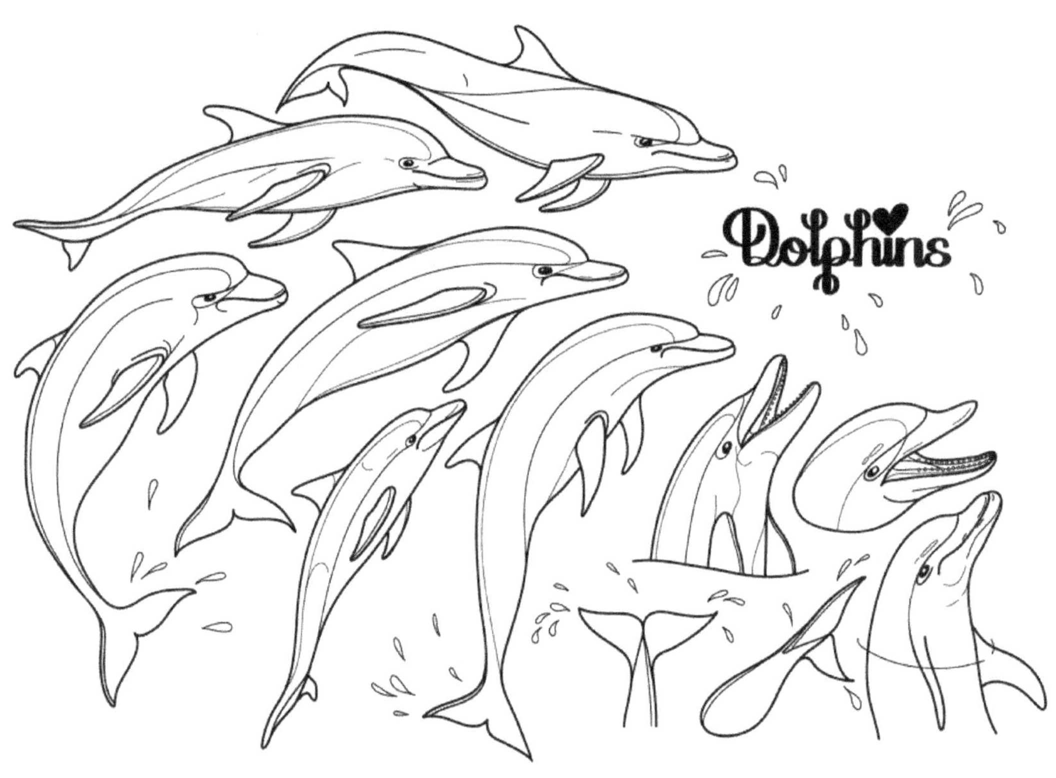
Dolphins

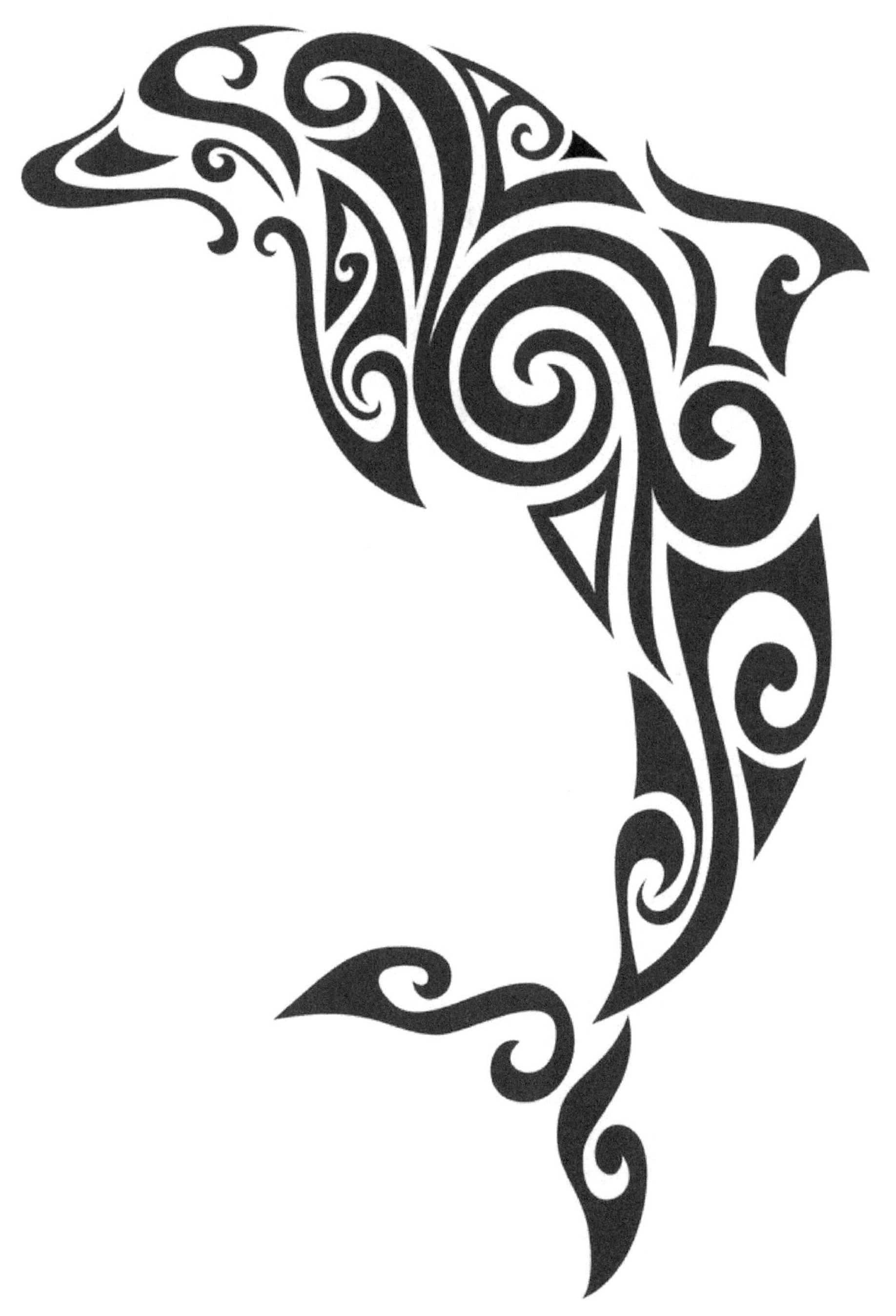

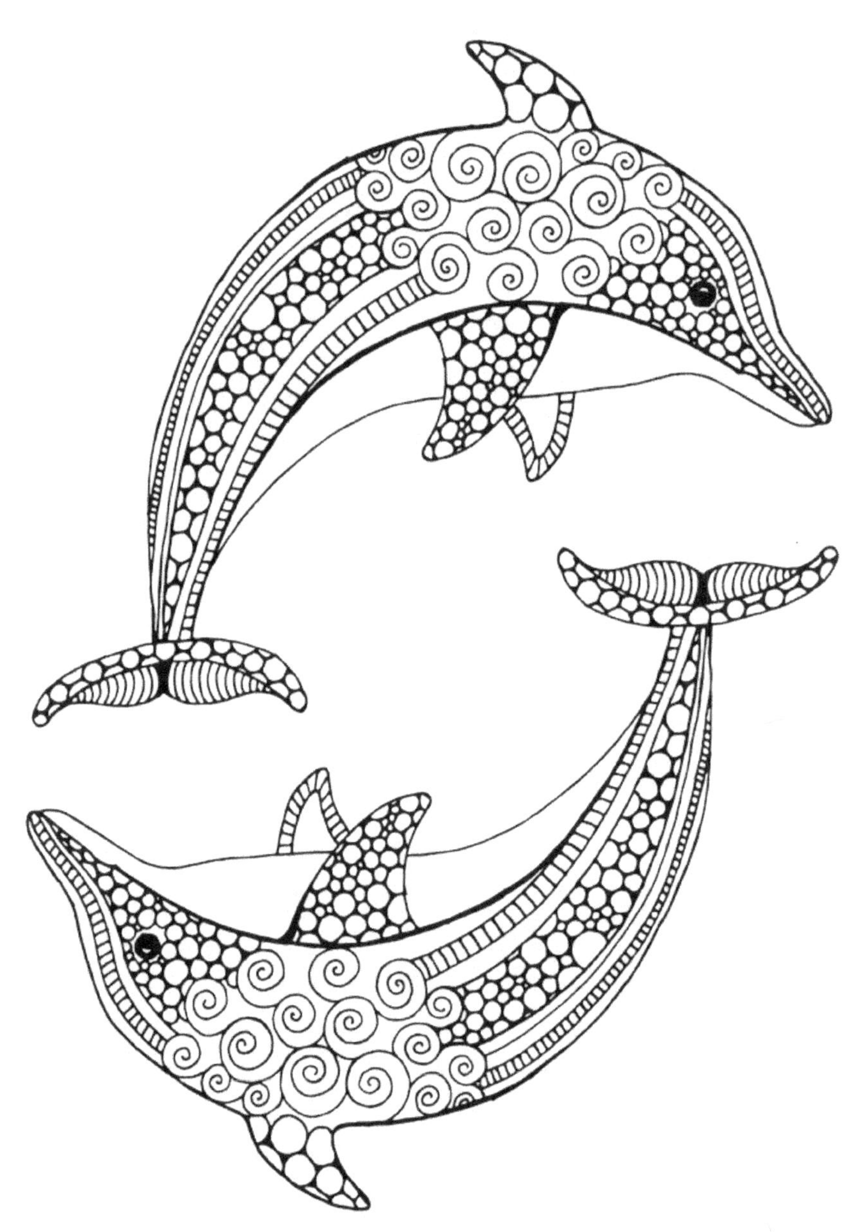

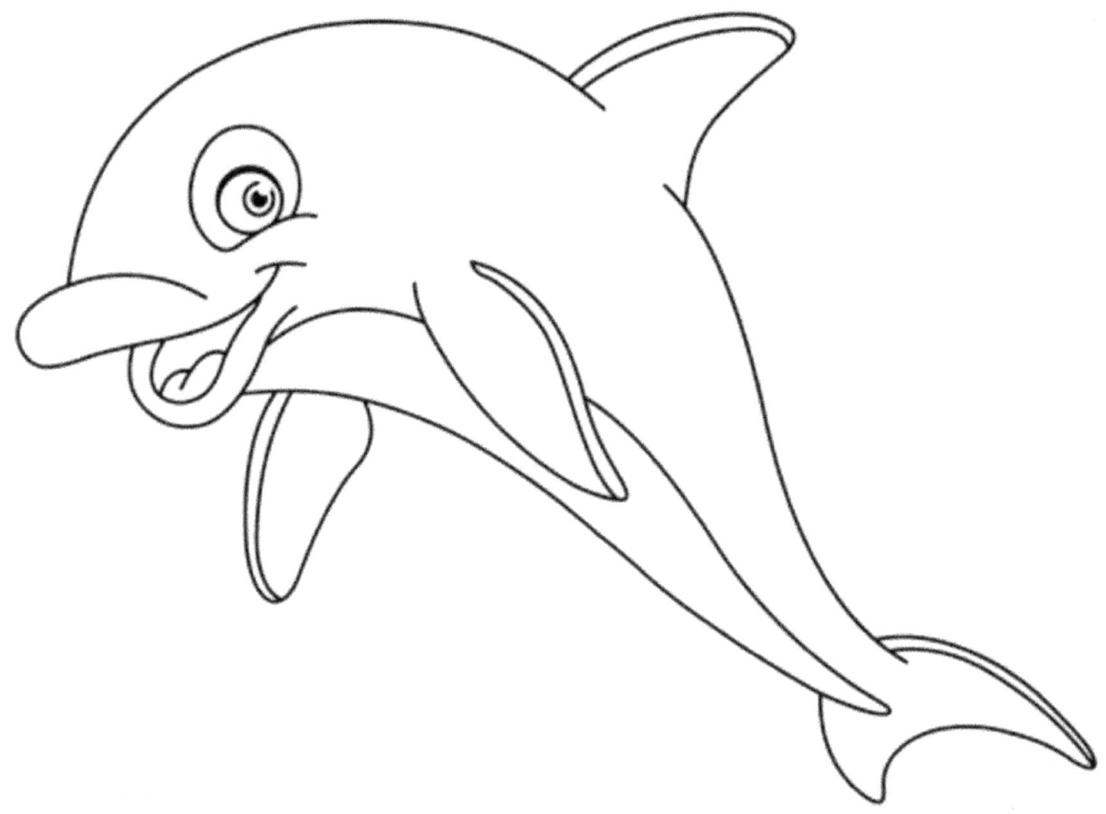